The Horse Soldiers' Raid

The Horse Soldiers' Raid

Grierson's Raid & Hatch's March During
the American Civil War

R. W. Surby

LEONAUR

The Horse Soldiers' Raid
Grierson's Raid & Hatch's March During the American Civil War
by R. W. Surby

First published under the title
Grierson Raids and Hatch's Sixty-Four Days March

Leonaur is an imprint of Oakpast Ltd

Copyright in this form © 2012 Oakpast Ltd

ISBN: 978-1-78282-018-5 (hardcover)
ISBN: 978-1-78282-019-2 (softcover)

http://www.leonaur.com

Publisher's Notes

Contents

To the officers and men,

who have so kindly assisted me in getting out this work,
and those who accompanied the various expeditions,

this work is most respectfully dedicated

by the

Author.

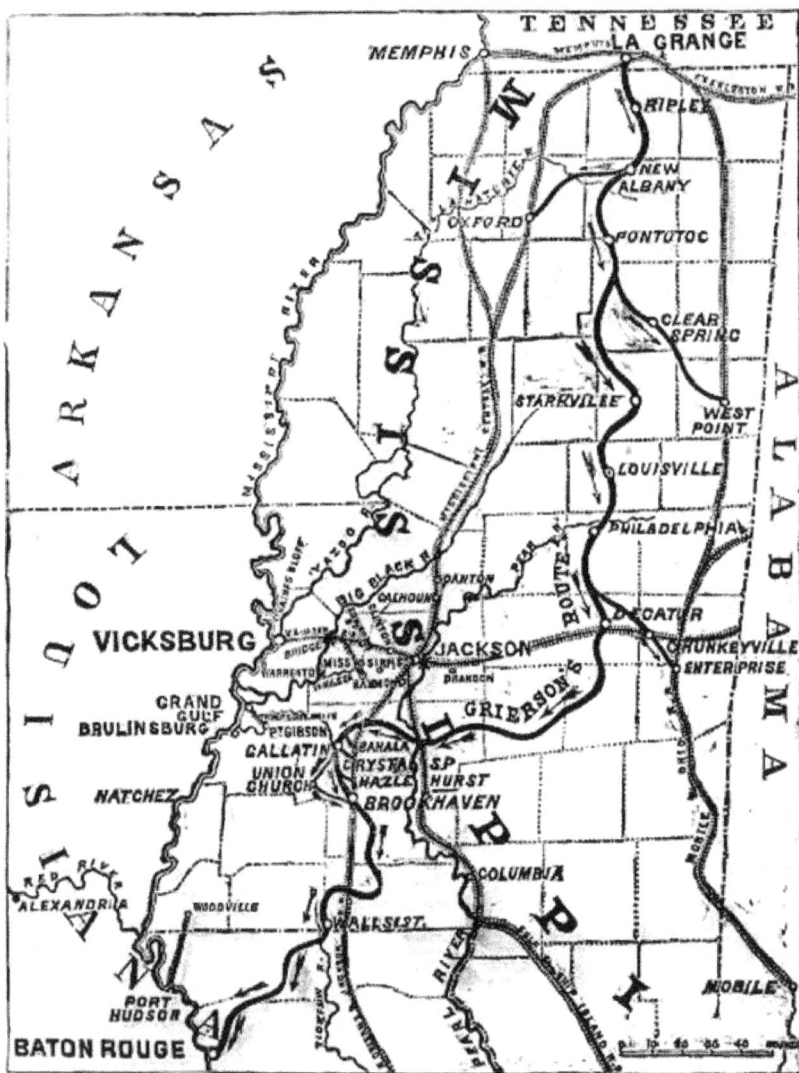

Colonel Grierson's route from La Grange to Baton Rouge

Preface

Dear Reader:—After waiting a sufficient length of time for some competent writers to place before the public the particulars of these world-renowned raids, and as yet nothing but imperfect reports have appeared in print, I therefore take the responsibility of offering to you the contents of my journal, together with items furnished by others. It was written under most embarrassing circumstances; just imagine yourself trying to write in an army tent, with six jolly comrades seated and standing around, talking and laughing on various subjects, (for soldiers like ladies gossip over the incidents of the day before retiring,) and you will need no other apology. Having performed a conspicuous part on the raid, I will try and furnish you with some items of a startling and amusing character, but nevertheless true.

Author.

Brig.-Gen. Ben. H. Grierson.

Grierson Raids

It was in the spring of eighteen hundred and sixty-three, that considerable emotion could be perceived in and about the camps of the Sixth and Seventh Illinois Cavalry regiments, also the Second Iowa, all of which were stationed at La Grange, Tennessee, on the line of the Memphis and Charleston railroad, fifty miles southeast of Memphis, at one time a very pretty, enterprising town, situated on a high ridge of land, commanding a fine view of the surrounding country; but this place, like many others of importance, has felt the effects of a civil war, and now presents a truly sad picture. It was upon this day that I shall commence my narrative.

"What's up?" is the question asked by a score or more of voices.

"A big scout, I reckon," is the general reply. A certain member is seen to emerge from headquarters, when the inquisitive ones gather around him.

"Come, John, tell us all about it; where are we going, and how long will we be gone?"

John's retreat being cut off, he replies as follows: "Now, boys, I'll tell you, but you must not say a word to any one, for it must be kept secret."

"Oh! no; we'll not tell; you know us."

"Well, boys, we are going on a big scout to Columbus, Mississippi, and play smash with the railroads."

"All right; we'll keep mum, and when we get to Columbus we'll make it pay." The sequel will show how correct John was in his opinion.

General W. S. Smith was at that time commander of the post, a gentleman and a soldier. The men had been complaining for more active service, or as they expressed it, "spoiling for a fight." General Smith finally announced to them, through their officers, that they should in

EDWARD PRINCE COL. 7TH RGT. ILL. VOL. CAV.

a few days have a chance to try their fighting qualities, which report was received with loud cheers; and a few days after this an order was issued to the commander of the first cavalry brigade to be ready for a march or scout, requiring all effective men, with five days rations in haversacks, with the understanding they were to last ten, and double rations of salt.

On the morning of the seventeenth of April, eighteen hundred and sixty-three, at an early hour, the following regiments left camp: the Second Iowa Cavalry, numbering between six and seven hundred men, rank and file, commanded by Colonel Edward Hatch, the Seventh Illinois Cavalry, numbering five hundred and forty-two, rank and file, commanded by Colonel Edward Prince, the Sixth Illinois Cavalry, with about five hundred men, commanded by Lieut.-Col. Loomis, and accompanied by Company K, First Illinois Battery, numbering six pieces light artillery, under the command of Captain J. B. Smith, the whole commanded by Colonel B. H. Grierson. Before proceeding further, I will state that Colonel Grierson planned this expedition some three months previous to this time, and it was submitted to General Hurlbut and remained null until again referred to by Colonel Grierson, when it was forwarded to General Grant, then near Vicksburg, who readily approved it, and sent suitable instructions how Colonel Grierson was to proceed.

The morning upon which the command moved out was a beautiful one, with a gentle breeze from the south. The fruit trees were all in full bloom, the gardens were fragrant with the perfume of spring flowers, the birds sang gaily, all of which infused a feeling of admiration and gladness into the hearts of all true lovers of nature. The men seemed to feel highly elated, and, as they marched in column of twos, some were singing, others laughing, while many were speculating as to our destination.

The following poetry I thought would express the feelings of the men at the time of our departure.

SONG OF THE FIRST BRIGADE.
The morning star is paling,
The camp-fires flicker low,
Our steeds are madly neighing,
For the bugle bids us go;
So put the foot in stirrup,
And shake the bridle free,

For today the fearless first
Are bound for Mississippi.

> *Chorus.*—With Grierson for our leader,
>   We'll chase the dastard foe,
>   'Till our horses bathe their fetlocks
>   In the Gulf of Mexico.

Our men are from the prairies,
That roll broad, proud and free;
From the loyal State of Illinois
And brave old Iowa;
And their hearts are open as their plains,
Their thoughts as proudly brave;
With Hatch for their commander,
They'll resist the rebel wave.

> *Chorus.*—Then quick into the saddle,
>   And shake the bridle free,
>   Today with gallant Grierson
>   We'll leave old Tennessee.

'Tis joy to be a trooper,
To fight for this free land,
'Tis joy to follow Grierson,
With his gallant, trusty band;
'Tis joy to see our Prince
Plunge like a meteor bright
Into the thickest of the fray,
And deal his deathly might.

> *Chorus.*—Oh! who would not be a trooper.
>   And follow Grierson's eye,
>   To battle for their country,
>   And, if needs be, to die.

By the many streams of water,
And the deep, murmuring shore,
On our soft, green peaceful prairies,
Our homes, we may see no more;
But in those homes our gentle wives,
And mothers, with silvery hairs,
Are loving us with tender hearts,
And shielding us with prayers.

Chorus.—*So trusting in our country's God,*
We draw our stout good blade,
For those we love at home,
And those who need our aid.

It is under such circumstances, with nothing to mar the feelings, that time passes swiftly away. The order of march for this day was to be as follows: Sixth Illinois Cavalry in advance. Through some mistake the Sixth took the wrong road near La Grange, was thrown to the west, and did not join the command until near camp, which was on the plantation of Dr. Ellis, four miles northwest of Ripley, Mississippi, distance from La Grange thirty miles. Just before going into camp five or six rebels were discovered crossing a field, and immediately a party was sent in pursuit, who captured three of them. Our advance met a young man who looked rather seedy; he was driving an ox team, and, unfortunately for him, wore a very good looking hat, which one of the boys took a fancy to and relieved him of, leaving the poor fellow looking rather sad. Colonel Prince, on coming up, noticed the man and inquired of him what was the matter; he stated his loss, when the colonel pulled out his pocket-book and gave him a two-dollar greenback, which seemed to please him very much.

SECOND DAY

Next morning, the eighteenth. At seven o'clock the command moved out, the Seventh Illinois in advance. At eight o'clock we passed through Ripley, in Tippah County, making a halt of one hour, then moved south towards New Albany. The day was delightful, and nothing occurred to interrupt the quiet prevailing, until we had marched four miles, when our ears were startled by the report of firearms. A party of eight rebels had fired on our advance, then retreated rapidly. A few shots were sent after them, no harm done to either side, and all became quiet again. Colonel Prince then detached the first battalion, under the command of Captain Graham, who took the direct route to New Albany, while the main column passed through Arizabee, crossing the Tallahatchie River two miles east of New Albany, arriving there at five o'clock, p. m.

Captain Graham arrived at the bridge near the latter place in time to prevent a rebel picket demolishing it. He had been there an hour when the main column arrived, and crossed in safety. Previous to leaving Ripley Colonel Hatch had been detached to move with his regiment eastward and southward, to cross the Tallahatchie about five miles above New Albany, with a view of rejoining the brigade some five or six miles below the latter place, (which Colonel Hatch accomplished with success). The Seventh Illinois captured this day four prisoners, two of Bartue's and two of Wetherall's men. The command camped for the night at Mr. Sloan's plantation, five miles below New Albany, a small place composed of a few dry-goods stores, whose stock needed replenishing; also some fine residences; altogether a pleasantly situated country town.

THIRD DAY

The morning of the nineteenth day was anything but agreeable, a heavy rain having fallen all night and continued the next morning until noon. At an early hour Colonel Prince, by order of Colonel Grierson, sent two companies of the Seventh Illinois, under command of Captain Trafton, back to the Tallahatchie, who drove a force of the enemy out of New Albany and rejoined the command at ten o'clock the same morning. Two companies of the same command being sent to the right to look after Captain Wetherall's (Confederate) company, which was camped in that vicinity, they had taken the hint and retired during the night. They however captured from Major Chalmers' command four prisoners, and destroyed some camp and garrison equipage. Two companies were also sent to the left to find some horses, said to be hid in the woods.

They returned to the column in a few hours, having had very poor success. The command left camp at ten o'clock in the morning. The road being slippery and muddy somewhat retarded our progress and damped our feelings. At a late dinner hour we stopped to feed, and while so doing some of the fortune-seeking ones were searching a house close by, in which they found concealed one keg of powder, several revolvers, and a few old United States muskets, which unfortunately resulted in the burning of the house and most of its contents. The officers made every effort to find the guilty party, but it occurred mysteriously, no one knew anything about it.

The Sixth Illinois, occupying the advance, entered Pontotac, county-seat of Pontotac County, at four o'clock, killing a rebel who persistently fired on the advance; (his name was Beers.) A small party of rebels were in town, when hearing of our advance skedaddled, leaving a wagon-load of ammunition and camp equipage which we destroyed. Captain Graham, of the Seventh Illinois, with three companies, found and destroyed between four and five hundred bushels of salt, (government property.) Pontotac is, or rather was before the war, a brisk business place, boasting a population of about three thousand inhabitants, a fine brick court-house, and beautiful residences, denoting wealth. After remaining about an hour we proceeded eight miles south, and encamped on the plantation of Mr. Wetherall, (brother of Captain Wetherall,) and Mr. Daggett. The whole command camped in sight of each other, having marched in the last two days sixty miles.

FOURTH DAY.

Next morning, the twentieth, at three o'clock, boots and saddles was sounded. Lieutenant Wilt and sixty men with a number of lead horses belonging to the Seventh Illinois, together with about the same number of the Sixth Illinois and Second Iowa, and one piece of artillery, all under the command of Major Love of the latter regiment, were sent back to Le Grange; the rest of the command, with the Second Iowa in advance, continued south passing through a good section of country somewhat rolling. The day being cloudy and damp, there was little interest displayed in viewing the country, and it was not until I had discovered that we had left the main road, and was making a new one through a wheat field of some extent; it was about six inches in height and of a beautiful green, which was a change from the mud; the question arose, what does this mean, and various were the conjectures.

The prevailing opinion was, that the enemy was near at hand, and we were on a flanking expedition, however, our fears were soon dispelled, the column had been conducted through the fields in order to avoid passing through the town of Houstan, leaving it on our right; a very pretty little place in Chickasaw County. Either the citizens had held out some inducements, or our commanders through a pure motive avoided marching the troops through, that pillaging might be avoided; there may have been some other motive, that of disguising our forces as much as possible—however, Houstan this time was favoured by a side view of our column, while house tops and church steeples presented a picturesque appearance to us, we proceeded on to Clear Springs and camped for the night, having marched forty miles.

FIFTH DAY.

Left camp on the morning of the twenty-first at daylight, the Seventh Illinois in advance; Colonel Hatch with the Second Iowa and one piece of artillery turned eastward from Clear Springs with orders to proceed toward Columbus, Mississippi, and destroy as much as possible of the Mobile and Ohio railroad, and make his way to Le Grange again. Some fears were felt for his success, as forces were concentrating in our rear, expecting to intercept us on our return, it was of the utmost importance that a feint should be made in the direction of Columbus in order to draw the enemies' forces that way and conceal the real movement which was then making all speed south. Colonel Hatch was just the officer to be entrusted with this perilous task, he accomplished the object but had some hard fighting, reaching our lines in safety. The Sixth and Seventh were now alone and various were the opinions expressed by the men as to our destination. The proceedings of the past few days showed that something was to be done; they felt equal to any task and, notwithstanding the heavy rain that was falling, they were cheerful and enlivened the march with songs and jokes.

The citizens were somewhat surprised to see so many "Yanks" so far down in "Dixie," and many were the questions asked,

"Where are you' ens all going to?"

Rebel couriers were ahead, and for several days our arrival was expected by them; they having had warning had concealed all of their valuable horses, mules, and negroes. Now the question will arise, how did we manage to subsist? Why, we just helped ourselves, or rather, when we stopped at a plantation to feed, a detail of men for guards was immediately made and stationed at the smoke-house, kitchen and dwelling house, with instructions not to allow anything to pass without permission of a commissioned officer, also a suitable person was appointed to issue out to the different companies a proper quantity of hams, shoulders, meal, and so forth, for one or two meals as the case required; this duty devolved upon William Pollard, commissary sergeant of the Sixth Illinois, he being the only representative of that department along, and fully competent to the task. Respecting the horses, it was seldom that there was any scarcity of corn and fodder, if there was not enough at one plantation, for the command, part went to the next, always keeping within supporting distance of each other.

Belonging to the non-commissioned staff I was a privileged character, and undoubtedly took many liberties not allowed me, consequently I had a good opportunity of observing many things, and learning some of the designs of our commanders. Possessed of a venturesome disposition I naturally wanted to be in the front, and it occurred to me I could do so; I immediately suggested my ideas to Lieut. Col. Blackburn (formerly my captain,) that of having some scouts in the advance dressed in citizens clothes, they could by proper

18

management gain much valuable information, although not without running some danger. Colonel Blackburn immediately had an interview with Colonel Grierson stating the object of the organisation; Colonel Grierson approved the plan provided the right men could be found, Colonel Blackburn said he knew just the men, and without further consideration, he had full permission to organize and control the scouts; it was not long before I was ordered to report to him, and was somewhat surprised when he requested me to act as scout, and take command of a squad of men.

This suited me, and without any hesitation I accepted the position with thanks, fully resolved not to abuse the confidence reposed in me. I received orders to take six or eight men, proceed at once on the advance and procure citizens dress, saddles, shot guns, and everything necessary for our disguise. It did not take long to do this, and by noon reported myself and men ready for duty; we excited some little curiosity and sold the Sixth Illinois boys completely, they thought we were prisoners and bored us with a thousand questions; after this we went by the name of "The Butternut Guerillas;" our old uniforms and carbines were placed in the hands of friends.

My instructions from Colonel Blackburn were to keep in the advance, from a quarter of a mile to two as the case required, to obtain all information respecting different roads, their destination, distance, and condition, also that of the streams, bridges, and the whereabouts of the enemy, their force, and was to exercise my own judgment in all cases where it required immediate action, to report to him or Colonel Prince from time to time. Another advantage was, that we would more easily find forage, and save trouble and delay by sending out squads for that purpose.

The advance guard each day being advised and cautioned about us, did not find or take us prisoners, and our signs were soon understood by both parties. We passed through Starkville, Ochtibleher County, and camped eight miles south of that place. Between Starkville and camp the scouts captured a lieutenant belonging to Vicksburg, who was seated in a fine buggy with a beautiful span of iron gray horses attached; the horses Colonel Grierson assigned to the battery. Also a mounted rebel was secured and taken along.

Sixth Day.

Morning of the twenty-second left camp at an early hour,—weather favourable. Before leaving camp Captain Graham of the Seventh, commanding a battalion, was sent to burn a Confederate shoe and saddle manufactory near Starkville; he succeeded in destroying several thousand pairs of boots and shoes besides a large quantity of leather and hats, capturing a quartermaster from Port Hudson, who was getting supplies for his regiment (the Twelfth Tennessee,) previous to leaving camp, the field officers had a consultation and were convinced that it was of the utmost importance to intercept and destroy the railroad and telegraph between Okalona and Macon, as near Macon as possible. This work Colonel Prince offered Captain Forbes, Company B, Seventh Illinois, whose company numbered thirty-five men and officers; Captain Forbes accepted at once, though he knew he would be obliged to repulse all attacks and travel at least fifty miles more than the command, would run great risk in being captured, as it was not known what force was at Macon, nor what force was following us; he was instructed, that if a force should be at Macon, to endeavour to cross the Ranox Bar and move toward Decatur, in Newton County, by the shortest route.

The captain proceeded on his perilous journey, and many feared that they would never see him again. The country through which we were passing was not of a prepossessing appearance—it was low and swampy. The scouts were quite successful during the day in finding several droves of horses and mules, with negroes concealed in the woods, to avoid being captured by our forces. The manner in which we obtained our information was quite easy in our assumed characters, when conversing with the hunters we passed ourselves off as confederates, belonging to commands in Tennessee; that we were ordered to keep in advance of the Yankies, watch their movements and when opportunity presented, to report to the nearest post; this story invariably was credited among them, and in a little while by ingratiating ourselves into their favour, we obtained their confidence, and was told where they had concealed their fine animals; I would then leave a man to inform the colonel when the column came up, and a squad of men would often bring in twenty-five horses and mules, with as many negroes, who would of their own accord accompany us.

I was very much amused one day; had taken three of my men with me and proceeded two miles from the main road expecting to find a Confederate captain at home, but he had left quite suddenly; found some good mules, upon which I mounted some negroes who were standing round with mouths wide open showing teeth like circular saws, at the sight of a Yankee, having never seen one before. On my return I passed a very fine residence—my attention was suddenly attracted by a motion made at one of the windows, I gave the order to halt; no sooner done than the front door flew open and three lovely looking females dressed in white appeared at the opening, their faces beaming with smiles, and in a voice soft and sweet invited us to dismount and come in. It was raining, we were all wet to the skin, and spattered with mud, contrasting strongly with the elegant appearance of everything around; I therefore begged to be excused as my time was limited, and we were watching the advanced movements of the Yankies; no sooner said than out they bounded, regardless of the rain, and coming to the gate were joined by an elderly lady who they addressed as mother, insisted upon our remaining over night. Various were the questions asked about the "Yanks" all of which we could answer satisfactorily; they informed us their father and brothers were in the Confederate Army.

One of the boys complained of being hungry; no sooner said than one of the ladies ran into the house, and soon returned with two black servants following, loaded down with eatables; we had to accept half a ham, that would make a hungry man laugh; biscuits, sweet cakes, fried sausage, and peach pie, all in abundance were pressed upon us, while one of the young ladies plucked some roses and presenting one to each bade us *adieu*, with many blessings and much success in our "holy cause;" on my way back I met a company of the Sixth Illinois, and cautioned them to still deceive the "ladies," and I presume it was some time ere they learned how bad they had been sold.

Another instance occurred where I visited a plantation, accompanied by two of my scouts. We found two young men at home, both belonging to the Confederate army. They were somewhat surprised to hear the Yankees were coming that way; all was excitement, the negroes were called up, and received orders to get all the horses and mules, and saddle two of them. We were invited into the house. Having told them that we would accompany them some distance, the demijohn was brought out, glasses placed upon the table, and a cordial invitation given to help ourselves to some "old rye," which invitation a soldier never refuses. The blacks soon announced all ready, and we started out, the young men armed with shotguns, eight negroes following with fourteen mules and six fine horses.

It was about one and a half miles to the road, upon which the column was advancing, and in the direction that we were going; when about half way I had a curiosity to examine their guns, which they seemed proud to exhibit; making a motion to one of my men he followed suit, thus we had them disarmed, and in a good humoured way informed them they were our prisoners; they laughed, thinking it a good joke, saying they were old soldiers, and not easily scared. We soon came in sight of the column, when our Confederate friends "smelt a rat," and with downcast countenances became uncommunicative. Shortly after this we passed through Whitefield, a small place of little importance.

After leaving this place the country began to look decidedly swampy, we were crossing the Big Black or Okaxuler River, which was much swollen by the recent rains. In many places we had to swim our horses and mules. Many troopers lost their animals and equipments, barely escaping with their lives. It was a tedious task piloting our way through this bottom, which extended in breadth nearly six miles, and was covered with water to the depth of three feet. You will ask how did we get our artillery over; this was accomplished by taking the ammunition out of the caissons, and packing it over our own horses, thereby keeping it dry. Unfortunately one of the gun carriages broke down, causing some delay, but through the ingenuity of Capt. Smith, commanding the guns, it was mounted next day on buggy wheels.

The Sixth Illinois cavalry succeeded in crossing and reached camp about two o'clock; the Seventh did not arrive until three the next morning. After leaving this dismal swamp, the country became more rolling, the roads were in better condition, vegetation more forward, and the citizens were impressed with the idea that we belonged to the rebel General Van Dora's command, and complimented us on our fine appearance, and said we were right good looking men. No couriers had preceded us on this road, and we enjoyed ourselves very much at the expense of the deluded citizens.

While passing a schoolhouse the teacher gave her pupils recess; the way they flocked to the roadside was not slow, hurrahing for Beauregard, Van Dora, and the Southern Confederacy. One little urchin imagined she recognized in one of the men an old acquaintance, and very impatiently inquired how John was, and if her uncle was along.

Before reaching Louisville the scouts captured a mail-coach containing the Port Hudson mail, together with some Confederate money, which was handed to Colonel Grierson. The letters were mostly in French, which was translated into English by Sergeant-Major Le Sure of the seventh; they contained some valuable information. Louisville is a neat little town of pretty location, in Winston County. After leaving it ten miles in our rear, we camped for the night, having travelled this day fifty miles. On this evening Captain Lynch of Company E, of the Sixth Illinois, and one of his men, Corporal W. H. H. Bullard, disguised themselves in citizens' dress, and started on a reconnoitring expedition towards Macon, with what success will appear hereafter.

SEVENTH DAY.

We left camp at an early hour and were now drawing near Pearl River Valley. A glance at the map will show the importance of this river on the Talla Hoga, and knowing it to be quite high from recent rains, and a possibility of news of our approach reaching them from other routes, it became necessary to secure the bridge. I was instructed to proceed rapidly and cautiously forward, and if possible, to secure it with my squad. When within two miles of the bridge, I met an old citizen mounted upon a mule. We passed the time of day and entered into conversation; he informed me that a picket was stationed at the bridge, composed of citizens, numbering five in all, his son being one of the party; all were armed with shotguns. They had torn up several planks from the centre of the bridge, and had placed combustibles on it ready to ignite on our approach.

I then wrote down the old man's name, and the whereabouts of his residence, which was on the opposite side of the river. He began to mistrust that all was not right, and says, "gentlemen you are not what you seem to be, you certainly are Yankees, for we got news in Philadelphia last night that 'you'ens' all were coming this way." I had now fully resolved upon scaring the old man into an unconditional surrender of the bridge. So, looking him in the face, I told him it now lay in his power to save his buildings from the torch, his own life, and probably that of his son, by saving the bridge. We started, and when within one half mile of our object we descended into a low bottom land, considerably flooded with water, making progress slowly.

Unless the enemy had a picket, or vidette, thrown out we could approach to within three hundred yards without being discovered. I now told the old man, who was trembling with fear, that he was to visit his friends, and tell them, that if they would surrender, they should not be harmed, but would be paroled as soon as we reached town, but if they did any damage to the bridge, his property would suffer for it.

The old man said he was confident of saving the bridge, but would not promise the surrender of his friends; that we cared nothing

23

about—the bridge was the important point. I impatiently followed the figure of the old man with my eye; when within a dozen yards of the bridge, he halted, and commenced telling his errand; but ere he had hardly half through, I could perceive some signs of uneasiness on the side of his listeners, they all at once jumped upon their horses and away they went. We then advanced to the bridge, replaced the planks, found two shot guns, that they had left in their flight, and leaving one man to wait for the column and turn the old man over to the colonel, I proceeded with the rest to Philadelphia.

This incident is mentioned as one of the many in which the *Power above* seemed shielding us from harm, as the destruction of the bridge would have been fatal to the expedition. In my case others might have acted differently; my object was to save life if possible, the bridge at all hazards. We now proceeded toward Philadelphia, occasionally firing a shot at some mounted citizen who were armed but took care to keep at a respectful distance. The nearer we approached the larger the force became in our advance, yet, they showed no disposition to come within range, until within about three hundred yards of town, when they were discovered drawn up in line across the road, upon which we were approaching.

I immediately sent a man back, requesting the commanding officer of the advance guard to send me ten men. I waited long enough to see they were coming, and turning to my men ordered them to charge, and as we neared them amid a cloud of dust, we commenced to discharge our revolvers at them, which had the desired effect of stampeding them; they fired but a few shots, and in a few minutes we had full possession of the town; resulting in the capture of six prisoners, nine horses with equipments. One of the prisoners being the county judge—a very worthy man. At first they evinced much uneasiness and thought their time was near to depart from this world. Colonel Grierson soon quieted their fears by telling them that he did not come among them to insult them, or destroy private property, that he was in quest of Confederate soldiers and government property. We left the Philadelphians in better humour and with a more favourable opinion of our intentions, and the conduct of our army.

The last I saw of them they were standing in line with arms extended perpendicular, and Colonel Prince was swearing them not to give any information for a certain length of time. Just as we were leaving Philadelphia, up came Captain Lynch and his corporal in disguise, having just arrived from their expedition to Macon, the particulars of which I obtained from Captain Lynch.

On his departure from Louisville he pushed through to Macon, travelling all night, arriving within half a mile of the place at eight o'clock next morning; travelling seventy-five miles, meeting with no trouble until halted by the picket in sight of the town; they demanded his business. The captain told them that he had been sent out from Enterprise to ascertain the whereabouts of the Yankees. "Why," says the guard, "you need not go any further, they are now within two miles of here. General Loring sent out a squad of cavalry to reconnoitre; they have all returned but one who is either killed or taken prisoner." The captain then inquired what force they had to defend the place, and was told that re-enforcements had arrived from Mobile— two regiments of cavalry, one of infantry, and two pieces of artillery. The captain made an excuse to withdraw by stating that he had left two men at a plantation about a mile from there; he would return for them and be back in a few hours. The guards thought it all right and allowed him to depart. The captain made good time, forfeiting his word to return.

After travelling all night and next day until about one hour of sunset, they reached the command, just as they were leaving Philadelphia. After proceeding seven miles south of the latter place the command halted to feed and rest for a few hours on the plantation of Esquire Payn. While so doing, at a council of the officers Lieut. Col. Blackburn offered a proposition, which was to take two hundred men and proceed to Newton Station, on the Southern railroad, to intercept the trains and destroy the track; his plan was favoured by Colonel Grierson, and at ten o'clock Colonel Blackburn started with the first battalion of Seventh Illinois. I was ordered by him to take two of my men and accompany him. The night was a beautiful starlight one, the roads in good condition, and meeting with no enemy, nothing occurred to interrupt the stillness that reigned until midnight, when the column was startled by the report of firearms, in the advance, which occurred in the following manner:

In coming to a point where the road forked, I was at a loss which one to take, and to decide the question, sent George Stedman back to a house to inquire, in the meantime I had advanced on the road leading to the right a short distance, and halted, with my horse standing crosswise the road, leaving a narrow neck of timber between me and the other road. Scout number two had preceded me a short distance, and was waiting by the shade of the timber. In a few minutes Stedman

25

came trotting back, and as he neared me I asked him if this was the right road; he did not seem to comprehend what I said but came up within a few feet of me and peering into my face a moment, without saying a word, wheeled his horse and galloped off. His actions puzzled me a little at first, and was giving no further thought to it, supposing he had gone back to the column with his information, when the first thing I heard was the report of firearms; though somewhat startled at first I did not move my position until the third shot had been fired, which impressed me with the idea that someone was firing at me, by hearing and seeing the fire-sparks fly from a stone the ball hit just beneath my horse's head, the next whizzed a few feet over me. I began to think it was time for me to get out of that, so I turned left about and retreated a few yards into the timber. Soon, *whiz, whiz*, came another shot, tearing through the timber; I immediately decided on a retreat, and went pell-mell through the scrub-oaks and briars for about two hundred yards, then coming to a halt, I heard another shot, then all was quiet again.

I now took time to think, and was of the opinion that we were ambushed from the point of timber between the two roads, and that the enemy had let us pass, and were firing into the advance of our column; still I could not account for the shots fired at me. I concluded to flank around and get to the column if possible. At that moment up came scout number two. We struck out and circled about a mile, striking the middle of the column, and soon learned that I was the sole object of all the firing. It appears that Stedman, when he rode up, did not recognize me, but hastily retreated to the fork of the road, and commenced firing at me with his revolver, causing the advance to hurry forward, who in turn began to fire with their carbines. Loss sustained, one hat. George was cautioned against firing upon his comrades again. It reminds me of the saying, "*better born lucky than rich.*"

When within four miles of Decatur I was ordered by Colonel Blackburn to take one of my men and proceed to the town and try and ascertain if there was any force stationed at Newton Station, their position; if any artillery, and any information I could obtain. We started, feeling secure of our disguise, and no couriers ahead to tell of our coming. About three o'clock in the morning we entered the quiet town of Decatur, in Newton County. No one was astir, the sleeping occupant little dreaming that two "Yanks" were treading on their sacred soil.

After going up and down, surveying all the streets, and satisfying ourselves that no one was astir, we halted in front of an old fashioned country inn, with its pigeon-hole windows standing halfway up the slanting roof. Dismounting and leaving my horse in care of my comrade, I stepped boldly up on the verandah, approached the door, knocked loudly; no answer. Repeated the summons; still no answer. Tried another door, with the same result. Began to think the hotel was evacuated. Made a forward movement, which proved the right one. After knocking at the door, a gruff voice on the inside inquired "who's there?"

I answered in a loud voice, "a Confederate soldier, on important business, in quest of information." In a moment the door opened, and an invitation to come in was extended, which I at once accepted, stepping into what appeared to be a sitting room and bedchamber in one.

I begged to be excused for disturbing them at so unseasonable an hour. No excuses were necessary. The old gentleman, who proved to be the proprietor of the establishment, scraped out a few coals in the fire place, which threw a lurid light across the room, drew forth a chair; and told me to be seated. At the same time he sprang into bed again, from beneath whose covering I could see a pair of sparkling, roguish black eyes, tresses black as the raven's wing, a mischievous mouth, belonging to a young and charming woman. Can it be possible, thinks I, that she is married to this old man. It must be so, for it is quite fashionable in the South, old husbands and young wives. My hospitable friend, in a mild tone, at once demanded my business. I told him in a few words.

Before answering me he was careful to ask me to whose command I belonged, where I came from, and why I was sent through there. I answered him by stating that I belonged to Van Dora's command, a portion of which was stationed at Columbus, Miss., and I was sent with a portion of them across the country to obtain all the information I could respecting a Yankee raid, which was then being made somewhere in the interior of the State, and supposed to be meditating an attack on the Southern railroad. I wished to know how far it was to any of our forces, at what points stationed, their strength, &c., as it was of the utmost importance that I should communicate to them.

This story seemed to satisfy the old gentleman. He then told me that the nearest force was at Newton Station, that our hospital was there, and about one hundred sick and wounded soldiers occupied it, and he was under the impression that two corps of infantry were stationed there. He also said that a considerable force of cavalry had passed a few days previous within five miles of Decatur, going east. He had heard the day before many conflicting reports about the Yankees, but had no idea that they would ever reach this far. Had he known that the "blue coats" were then within rifle shot, that dreaded disease, the "cholera," would not have caused more consternation in town. My partner called me. A sweet voice invited me to call if I came that way again. I promised, and, bidding goodbye, left them to slumber.

I met the column just entering the town, reported to Colonel Blackburn, and again assumed my place in front. It was not long after leaving this town that streaks of daylight began to appear in the east, and a glorious sun arose to crown the day.

EIGHTH DAY.

The eighth day found us passing through a timbered country somewhat rolling, and displaying but little cultivation. Decatur is a small place in Newton County. It being night, I could see but little of the town. When within five miles of Newton Station Colonel Blackburn ordered me to proceed lively with my two men to the station, reconnoitre, and report what force was stationed there, what time the train would arrive, and so forth.

This suited us. On we went, meeting with no obstacles, approached to within half a mile of town, found an elevated position, from whence I could obtain a pretty good view of the place; could not see any camp; saw several persons walking and standing around a large building, which I took to be the hospital. I felt pretty well satisfied that there was no force stationed there, or we would have seen their pickets ere we approached so close to town.

I told the men we would proceed and see a little more before reporting. We started leisurely along and stopped at a house just at the edge of town; found a white man, called for a drink of water, and asked him how long before the train would be in. He said it was due in about three quarters of an hour. I ascertained that no force was stationed here. Was obtaining other information, when my ears were startled by the whistle of a locomotive. It seemed a long way off. I then inquired what train that was. The man said it was the freight train coming from the east, due at nine o'clock, a. m.

I now allowed there was no time to lose in order to capture the train. The column must be here. I at once sent back one man to tell the colonel to hasten with all speed or lose the train. I then, with my scout, made for the depot to secure the telegraph, but found, upon reaching there, no office. By this time the convalescents began to pour out of the hospital, (which building stood within one hundred yards of the depot) to see who and what we were. I knew the column would be here in a few minutes, and, with revolver in hand, approached it and told them to remain inside, not to come out on peril of their lives.

In a moment the column came charging down the street, which was immediately picketed to prevent any one leaving town. The horses were led back behind the buildings, and one man sent to each switch, to lay concealed until the train passed, then to spring forward and alter it. Every "blue coat" was ordered to lay behind the buildings until the train was secured. On she came, puffing and blowing with the weight of twenty-five cars, loaded with railroad ties, bridge timber and plank. In a few minutes this train was in our possession and switched on a side track. Another train would be due in a few minutes from the West. Men were placed near the switches. The command was ordered to hide themselves from view, and everything was perfected just as the whistle sounded.

On she came rounding the curve, her passengers unconscious of the surprise that awaited them. The engineer decreased her speed. She was now nearly opposite the depot. Springing upon the steps of the locomotive, and presenting my revolver at the engineer, told him if he reversed that engine I would put a ball through him. He was at my mercy, and obeyed orders. It would have done anyone good to have seen the men rush from their hiding places amid the shouts and cheers which rent the air of "the train is ours." It contained twelve freight cars and one passenger car, four loaded with ammunition and arms, six with commissary and quartermasters' stores, and two with dry goods and household property belonging to families moving from Vicksburg.

Several passengers were aboard, and as soon as they learned what was up, commenced throwing out of the windows on the opposite side from us their valuables, which fell into the water, it being low and swampy on that side of the track. A few revolvers, some papers and a considerable amount of money was unceremoniously thrown out. Some of the men, who never let anything pass unobserved, accidentally picked up a few articles. One old watch, which was floating on the water, contained about eight thousand dollars in Confederate "greenbacks."

This train being switched off on the side track with the other, the private property thrown out, fires were kindled in each car. The whole soon became one continuous flame. By eleven o'clock the heat had reached the shells, which began to explode, and must have sounded at a distance like a sharp artillery duel. Such was the impression it had on Colonel Grierson and the rest of the command, who were eight miles in our rear, following us up. As soon as they heard the reports of the bursting shells, they allowed that Colonel Blackburn was attacked, and the order was given, "trot, gallop, march," and on they came, expecting battle, but instead, found the men had charged on a barrel of whisky, which they were confiscating. I did not see a man that had more or less than a canteen full.

As soon as Colonel Grierson came up, two battalions, under command of Major Starr, of the Sixth Illinois, was sent to destroy the bridges and trestle-work for six miles on the east side of the station, while one battalion of the seventh, under command of Captain Hening, destroyed them the same distance on the west, also effectually destroying the telegraph lines for some distance. A building was found containing a large quantity of United States rifles and clothing which was burned. Seventy-five prisoners were captured and paroled, (which duty devolved upon Adjutant George Root, 7th Illinois). One depot, two locomotives and all the cars, everything was destroyed. Colonel Blackburn was highly complimented for his success.

Everything being completed, rally was sounded, men fell into line, and at two o'clock, p.m., the command moved forward. Passing the railroad we proceeded south, which pleased the men very much. In justice to them I will mention that while at the railroad station they allowed the patients of the hospital to supply themselves with sugar, coffee and clothing before destroying it. It was now useless to disguise our character further; the news of "Yanks" was too far ahead. Couriers were going in all directions, spreading various reports respecting our strength. Some had estimated it as high as fifteen hundred, and some as many thousand; that we burned all the towns, insulted the females, and shot and hung all defenceless old citizens.

It was very annoying to listen to the stories repeated by many that we captured during the day; and many was the load of bacon, flour and household goods and valuables that we captured, which the poor deluded owners were trying to run off from the "Yanks," deserting their mansions, leaving all to the mercy of the invaders.

Great credit is due the commanders of this expedition for their efforts to prevent the destruction of private property, and the men for abstaining from destruction, which they could have done quite easily. It now required more energy and perseverance on the part of the scouts; the rumours ahead were contradictory, and the designs upon us, hard to tell; the roads must be found, so that there should be no delay to the column, at the same time, through our assumed character, find all the horses we could, and get them, or give information to the command where they could be found. The roads being good, we made good time, passing through Garlandville, where we found the citizens organized, armed and ready to receive us; they fired on the advance, wounding one man and killing one horse; we charged them, capturing nearly the entire party.

They were all aged men and very much alarmed, supposing that we would murder them and their families, burn their homes, and commit other unheard of outrages. We disarmed them and quieted their fears by releasing them, assuring them that we had come among them not to make war upon defenceless women and children but upon the armed rebels; they appeared elated at what they deemed their good fortune, and one old man ventured to remark that hereafter his prayers should be for the Union Army.

The column stopped to feed on the plantation of Mr. Bender, twelve miles from Newton Station. After two hours' rest we started again, feeling somewhat old and tired. We would occasionally see citizens dodging about, watching but avoiding us; we would sometimes give chase, but they escaped in the by-paths.

We continued our journey this night, through timber land. I was so sleepy that, after trying all in my power to keep awake, and finding I could not, I dropped back to the column, and was aroused several times; but it was no use, sleep I must have, and sleep I got, for when I awoke I found that my horse was nibbling the grass, and I was on the eve of taking a somersault over his head. I was alone, and, reader, I was awake at once; not a sound could I hear. The night was intensely dark and dreary, and the shade from the timber made it dismal enough. It was only a moment before I acted. I could not see anything of the road, so I dismounted and commenced feeling for it; I found it several yards to my left. To get on the right course was the next thing; this I did by feeling for the toe and heel of the horse-shoe prints. Mounting my trusty steed I put him on the track, with a slack bridle and smart canter, trusting to his instinct to keep the road. After travelling about two miles I was rewarded by overtaking the rear-guard to the column. I assure you I felt relieved.

My horse was seen to turn out from the column, but supposing I had left the column purposely, to fix something about my saddle, which is nothing unusual on a march, besides the men were so sleepy and tired that nothing but a shot fired would arouse them. I found that I was no sooner out of one danger—that of being captured—than I was into another. When within one mile of camp, and as the column was passing a plantation, my attention was attracted to a barn-yard, where were apparently some fine horses. A wide lane extended between the barn-yard and house. I proceeded up the lane a short distance, hitched my horse to the fence and sprang over into the yard, and joined in the chase after a fine cream coloured horse.

While thus engaged an officer belonging to the Sixth Illinois rode up the lane, and seeing my horse with citizen's saddle and shot gun attached to it, concluded that some guerillas were around, and was calling for some of his men, who did not appear to be there; he continued to ride back and forth. My chase after the steed proving unsuccessful, I was returning to my horse, when I discovered the officer, as described; my first impulse on seeing him, which was a very indistinct view, was that he was a Rebel, and without further investigation I drew my revolver, jumped on the fence presenting it at him, demanded his surrender, or I would fire; he had his revolver in his hand, but dare not raise it for fear of my putting my threat into execution, which I certainly should have done, had he made any show of resistance.

Just at this stage of the game, when I was going to order my prisoner to drop his arms, I was startled by the report of firearms just in my rear, at the same time I felt a stinging sensation on my left side. I was hit, and like a flash the thought occurred to me, that I was fired on by one of my own men; and still keeping my men in view, I shouted, I am one of the Seventh, what are you firing at me for; this explained all; the person who fired was William Pollard, commissary sergeant of the Sixth; the moment I spoke he knew my voice.

"Why," says he, "sergeant—that is Captain Skinner, of the Sixth; but, my God, you are hit."

"Yes," I replied, "I am; but it is nothing serious."

It turned out that the sergeant knew the captain, but my back being turned toward him, and my clothes being decidedly "butternut," he came to the same conclusion respecting my character that I had that of the captain.

They allowed it was a good joke, but I could not view it in that light, but in my heart I thanked God that it was no worse. Upon examining my side I found that the ball had ruffled the skin for about three inches just over my hip (for a few days it burned and smarted considerable.) We repaired to camp, which was a short distance from there. It was eleven o'clock, and for the first time in forty hours did we take off our saddles from our weary horses.

NINTH DAY.

On the morning of the twenty-fifth, we left camp at eight o'clock; the sky obscured by clouds indicating rain. Our progress was impeded by the bad roads; the country was thinly settled, and we had to swim our horses across the streams. Being considerably in advance, I stopped at a plantation, the appearance of which did not denote much wealth; a double log-house, and a few outbuildings. On approaching the stoop I was met by five females, who betrayed in their countenances, much uneasiness and fear—the cause was soon explained.

I at once inquired if there was any men about, and with one voice they all replied, "No sir, our husbands are all in the army of Vicksburg."

"And so, ladies, you are all married?"

"Yes, sir; is there anything strange about that."

"Oh no," I replied, laughing, "only it is strange to see so many married ladies at one house." To this they replied, that they had met to sympathize with each other. I then asked them for a drink of milk; they said that they had none, but would bring some water, which we accepted with thanks; one of the number, an old lady, wanted to know how soon this cruel war was going to end.

I concluded to utter a few Union sentiments, to see with what effect they would be received. I answered her by saying, that I thought it would stop just as soon as the old Stars and Stripes floated triumphantly over all the South. Looking at me with some surprise pictured in her countenance, she said, "I always did like that old flag, and I think this 'ere war all wrong, and if it had'nt been for these big lamed folks, we'd all be living in peace. There's my husband, he'd no lawing nor law-suits in court, but minded his own business, and had nothing to do making this war; but they had to come and conscript him, and take him off to Vicksburg, and I don't expect to see him agen—after being together for thirty-six years to be parted this way—" the tears trickled down her cheeks as she continued, "I suppose you are conscripting; well, you'll find no men around here; you'd better conscript all the women too; we have no one left to care for us; we don't own any blacks."

By this time I began to think there were still some sparks left burning for the old Union—that they were not all extinguished by the adulterated fluids of secession, and finally I asked the old lady what she thought about the "Yanks."

"Well," says she, "we've hearn a heap about them that wasn't good, and I've hearn tell a heap about them that was right smart in their favour. I've never seen but one, that is Mr. P——, who lives four miles from here; he came all the way from Ohio, and is a good man."

"Now, madam," says I "what would you think if I should tell you that we were Yankees?"

Picking me up before I had scarcely finished the sentence, she replied, "Now, young man, just stop that thar kind of talk; I aint going to be fooled in that thar way; you aint no Yankees, and you can't make me believe it, and I aint going to tell you a word about where the men are." By this time I looked up the road and saw the column advancing. I beckoned the old lady to me, and pointing to them told her they were all Yankees, "and, my good woman, we are Yankees, too."

The old lady's eyes opened to their widest extent, and turning around she raised her hands in a praying attitude, said "good Lord deliver us! what will we'uns all do;" and calling the "gals," as she termed them, showed them the column. At first they felt very much alarmed; we soon quieted their fears, and assured them that they were perfectly safe.

We were called into the house, and in a few minutes pies, bread, butter and milk in abundance was placed upon the table, and we were invited to help ourselves. While so doing the old lady was pulling an old chest from under the bed, and soon displayed to us a good sized flag, representing that good old flag for which we were fighting, and to protect its beautiful folds, so that it may continue to wave

O'er the land of the free,
And the home of the brave.

This was sufficient to satisfy me that the old lady was all right on the Union question; at the same time one of the other ladies expressed a wish that "John and William only knew what we were, how soon they would come out of the woods." I left the old lady wishing that God, in his mercy, would spare her husband, and that peace would soon be permanently restored to our afflicted country; then she need no longer keep concealed the "banner of liberty," which, though—

Thousands of true and brave,
Their heroic lives may end;
O'er thousands that flag shall wave,
Thousands its folds defend.

And as I journeyed on I thought how many of our readers, were they to take a trip through the interior of Mississippi, would be most bitterly disappointed; where they expected to find educated minds, elegant mansions, beautiful fields, quiet retirement luxuriating in wealth, they would find a double log cabin or frame house, with plain furniture (very scant), a feint show of comfort, a little garden spot, profuse with flowers of various hues (not very tastefully arranged), fields that show a lack of proper cultivation. Altogether, there is no show of wealth. And as for the high-toned intellect, with few exceptions, it is not to be found. Many words they express have the negro accent, and their knowledge of the geography of our country, its population, and resources, is very deficient.

No free schools to educate their children, and not sufficient wealth to send them from home, they continue in ignorance—so I thought as a pretty girl of some eighteen summers remarked one day as we were passing, "why, ma, they all look like we'uns do." Their minds prejudiced, they will continue to be the tools and dupes of the educated classes, who are building up their hopes on establishing a monarchical government; but when the time arrives that these prominent leaders are brought before the bar of justice, and their evil designs frustrated, and our country cleansed of those evils, then will knowledge flow like lava into the minds of those who now think there is no soil equal to that which raises cotton.

We passed through Pineville—a small place—and at noon stopped at a plantation and fed. The proprietor was absent—about a mile from the house, with his slaves, cultivating corn. I was ordered by Colonel Blackburn to go and request him to come to the house. I found him, as I expected, with a large leather-bound whip. He was seated on a stump, from which he commanded a view of the negroes, about twenty-five, male and female. I approached him, and passed the time of day; he did not seem at all surprised to see me, and at once asked me what success I had hunting, and how Pemberton was getting along at Vicksburg. I answered that I thought the latter place was safe against the whole Northern army; but as for hunting, I was not on that kind of business; that there was a large force of us up at his house, and I

35

was sent to request him to come up. He at once called an old negro, giving him his whip, and instructing him what to do. We started, he on foot, I mounted.

While on the way he asked me whose command I belonged to, and where we were going. I told him we belonged to "Williams'" command, late from Tennessee, but now from Jackson, Miss., and were in quest of commissary stores, and picking up deserters and conscripts. As we came in sight of his barn-yard he was perfectly astonished to see so many troops; but what worried him the most was that they had all helped themselves to his corn and fodder, without asking his permission—besides he had none to spare; not but what the Confederate vouchers were good enough, and he was willing to loan his share, that he had fed several squads, but he did not have more than he wanted for his own use. As we passed through among the men he remarked how well they were dressed, how healthy they looked, and what fine arms we had. I told him we were the best equipped cavalry in the Confederate service, and had been in several battles. I entered the house with him, and not letting him have an opportunity to talk with his wife, ushered him into the room occupied by Colonel Grierson and other officers.

I at once introduced the colonel to him as "Colonel Williams, from Jackson, Mississippi, formerly from Tennessee," at the same time intrusting to the colonel that our friend could give information of deserters, conscripts and provisions, which hint was sufficient for those present. I then withdrew, to lay down and rest my weary limbs upon the verandah. Considerable information was obtained from this planter. While here some of the men found a negro imprisoned in a log-hut, with manacles fastened about both ankles, and a chain attached to it, fastened to a ring in the floor. Colonel Blackburn had the irons cut off, and it was a sickening sight to look at those ankles; the flesh was worn off to the bone and almost in a state of mortification; the rings that went around the ankle were one inch in thickness, the whole weighing about twenty-five pounds. The poor fellow felt quite grateful, and never once complained about his scars. He accompanied us through to Baton Rouge. His only offence for all this treatment was trying to run away from bondage.

Just as the shades of night began to set in we halted and camped on the plantation of Dr. D———. Information had been obtained that a force of "rebs" were making their way from Mobile to intercept us. It was necessary that we should know something about their movements and force. About nine o'clock, after holding a consultation, Colonel Grierson requested Colonel Blackburn to select one of the scouts and report with him. In a few minutes Colonel Blackburn appeared with scout Samuel Nelson, of the Seventh Illinois. He was then instructed to proceed due north to Forest Station, thirty miles from where we were camped, and cut the telegraph line between Jackson and Meridian, on the Southern railroad, and if successful, bring a piece of the wire, as proof of its accomplishment; and if he had time to fire the bridge before daylight to do so, if not return to the command.

After being supplied with a quantity of Confederate money, Samuel started on his perilous journey. After proceeding sixteen miles he met a force of Rebel cavalry, about eighteen hundred strong. He was halted and asked who he was and what he was doing here. He replied that he had been "pressed in" by the "Yanks" and compelled to guide them; that they kept him two days, releasing him the day before on a parole; that he was then on his way to a friend, residing at Forest Grove. He was then asked what force the Yankees had and where he left them. He replied that he had left them the day before at noon near Garlandville; that their force was about eighteen hundred men, well armed, enough, he thought, to whip them. He was then asked the nearest route to Garlandville, and which course the Yankees went from there.

Sam directed them so as to lead them away from the proper trail, telling them the Yankees had left before he did and gone in the direction of the Mobile railroad. Apparently satisfied with the information they started, allowing Samuel to pursue his journey. After he thought they had gone far enough he turned about, retraced his steps about one mile, then taking a right-hand road, and pressing in a negro as guide, reached camp about five o'clock the next morning. This valuable information was at once conveyed to Colonel Grierson, who decided on evacuating immediately. Boots and saddles was sounded, and the command moved out at once. It was a fortunate thing that this scout was sent out, as there would have been a force upon us by daylight that would have annoyed us to some extent. As it afterwards proved, they were thrown two days in our rear. The telegraph project was abandoned.

TENTH DAY.

Left camp at five o'clock—the Sixth Illinois in advance. Three soldiers had to be left behind this morning, they being too feeble to travel further. About eight o'clock we passed through Raleigh, Smith County, a small place having rather a deserted appearance. On entering the place I discovered a man hastily mounting his horse and riding away at full speed, which looked rather suspicious; he was requested to halt, but paying no attention, kept increasing his speed. I told two of my men to give him chase; they being well mounted soon came up within pistol shot of him, when a few shots fired convinced him that there was danger in his rear, he concluded to halt, and very reluctantly returned to town, where he was delivered over to Colonel Grierson, together with five thousand Confederate "greenbacks," and a bundle of papers; he proved to be the county sheriff, and possessed some valuable information.

During the day we travelled through considerable pine timber plantations, few and far between. We experienced some scarcity of forage. It was just about dusk when I stopped at a plantation to dry my clothes, it having rained all the afternoon; had a very lively conversation with the proprietor who proved to be another sheriff (but minus the five thousand,) one that had no little conceit of his own abilities; he imagined we were hunting up deserters, and did not trouble himself to ask our business particularly, not half so much as we did to try the quality of his home made whisky, which he very generously supplied.

Imagine his astonishment when I ordered his negro servant to bring his masters horse to the door without delay, at the same time allowing the sheriff permission to procure a change of clothing, which he crammed into his saddle bags with an oath, exclaiming that it was d——d strange that he should be ordered round in his own house in this style, that he was not subject to conscription, and he be d——d if somebody should not have to pay for this trouble. He did not seem well posted in military matters. By this time up came the column, and Mr. Sheriff was introduced to Colonel Grierson, under the impression that he was in the presence of some noted general in the Confederate army. He was ready to tell all he knew, and more too.

We were now nearing Stony River and near Westville, in Simpson County, when the column was overtaken by two messengers from Captain Forbes, who then about thirty miles in our rear, requesting us not to burn any more bridges, as he was endeavouring to overtake us. This was joyful news to us. One of the messengers, whose name is Wood, was one of the scouts, and had rendered much valuable assistance on the expedition that was now trying to reach us, of which

I will speak hereafter. About nine o'clock the Sixth Illinois camped on the plantation of Major ——; the Seventh, going a mile further, crossed Stony River bridge and camped at Mr. Smith's plantation. The rebel major was quietly seated in his house, when Colonel Grierson halted before it. Coming out he wished to know whose command this was. No one seemed to pay any attention to him, but riding in through his gate into his garden, dismounting and hitching their horses to the beautiful shade trees.

This was more than he bargained for, and he foamed and tore around, swearing that it was an insult upon his dignity, and he'd be d——d if he would not report the commanding officer to General Pemberton; he would not stand such abuse and insult on his own premises; his garden was ruined, and they were feeding up all of his corn and fodder. The major learned his mistake before morning, respecting our character, and had nothing more to say about his garden. Distance marched this day forty-two miles. Though tired and sleepy, there were those who did not rest or sleep longer than to feed their horses and prepare supper. As the citizens were arming themselves, and, the news was flying in every direction, it was a matter of life or death that Pearl River should be crossed and the New Orleans and Southern railroad reached, without any delay.

So thought Colonel Prince; and acting on the impulse he had an interview with Colonel Grierson, and obtained permission to move directly forward, and with two hundred picked men of his regiment to secure the ferry across Pearl River before the enemy should destroy it. The following companies were detached: I, C, E and L. The distance to the river was thirteen miles, and from thence to Hazelhurst Station twelve miles. The remainder of the two regiments were to come forward as soon as they were sufficiently rested. The colonel left with the four companies at two o'clock on the morning of the twenty-seventh. Some of the scouts accompanied him, they being permitted to sup.

ELEVENTH DAY.

At daylight the remainder of the command moved out, and it was discovered that Mr. Sheriff number two had effected his escape during the night, and availed himself of a fine horse belonging to one of Colonel Grierson's orderlies. Taking the advance I reached Pearl River, and found that Colonel Prince had succeeded in crossing about one hundred of his men. He had reached the bank of the river before daylight, and, contrary to the information he had received, the flat-boat was upon the opposite side. Not daring to arouse any of the citizens, the colonel called for a volunteer, who, with a powerful horse, undertook to swim the river; but the rapidity of the swollen stream carried him far below the landing, where there was quicksand, and he barely escaped to the shore with his life; his name was Henry Dower, company I, Seventh Illinois.

A few minutes later a man from the house came down toward the river, and, with North Carolina accent, wanted to know if we wished to cross, to which the colonel replied, in a very fair imitation of the same tongue, that a few of us would like to get across, and it was harder to wake his negro ferrymen than to catch the d——d conscripts. The proprietor apologized, and woke up his ferrymen, who brought the boat across, from which time it remained in federal possession. For all the proprietor knew it was in the possession of the first regiment Alabama cavalry, from Mobile. The colonel says the breakfast he gave the first Alabama will long be highly appreciated. The importance of this dispatch in this instance was proved half an hour later, by the capture of a courier, who was flying to the ferry with the news that the "Yanks" were coming, and that the ferry must be destroyed immediately.

By the time that Colonel Prince had crossed his two hundred men the rest of the command came up, having left a guard at Stony River bridge to await the arrival of Captain Forbes. It was known that a rebel transport was some seven miles up the river, that carried two pieces, six-pounders. Colonel Grierson sent a detachment of men two or three miles above the ferry, where they could lay behind the river bank, secure from artillery, and engage the transport if she attempted to come down; but she did not make her appearance, probably apprehending capture. Leaving the rest of the command crossing—a slow, tedious task, as only twenty-four horses could go at a time Colonel Prince with his two hundred men proceeded toward Hazelhurst. The scouts were ordered ahead, and had not advanced more than four miles before we began to pick up citizens, who were collecting together and arming themselves to repel the invader.

One small man, with sandy whiskers and foxy eyes, trying to look as savage as a meat-axe, had secured in an old belt around his waist two large old flint-lock dragoon pistols, and slung over his shoulder a large leather pouch and powder-horn, and on his left shoulder, with his hand resting on the stock, and old United States musket, flint-lock. As I came up to him he brought his gun to a carry arms, and between a grin and a laugh exclaimed: "They is coming, capting, and I am ready; I've jist bid the old woman goodbye, and told her that she need not expect me back until I had killed four Yankees, and they were exterminated from out our Southern *sile*; I'm good for three of them, anyhow; I've been through the Mexican war, and know how to use them ere weapons."

I gave the men the wink, which they understood, and approaching the "exterminator" began to compliment him on the appearance of his arms, and requested to look at them. Without any hesitation he passed over his musket to me; the other men in the meantime had his pistols. I informed him he was a prisoner, and would soon have a chance to see the general. Leaving him with one of the scouts, to be turned over to the colonel, I proceeded some two miles further, when I saw some ten or twelve men together, some of them mounted, while others were standing and sitting on some pieces of timber. We boldly advanced, and when within speaking distance I discovered there was a small building, and further that it was a gunsmith's shop, on rather a small scale.

A few questions were asked by the crowd respecting the "Yanks," which were answered by letting them know that they were supposed to be advancing toward Pearl River. They had flocked here with their old shot-guns, muskets, rifles and pistols, some of which looked as if they were made in the year one. Taking them all prisoners, which somewhat surprised them, we proceeded into the shop and threw out twenty-five guns, of all descriptions; taking them one at a time and striking the stock on the ground, breaking them off at the breech, then taking the barrel and putting one end under some weighty substance and giving it a jerk or two, it was no longer fit for anything but to shoot around corners. These prisoners were turned over to the column.

When within four miles of Hazelhurst, Colonel Prince handed me a written dispatch and ordered me to send two of my men with it to the station, to be handed to the telegraph operator. I at once hastened forward and sent Stedman and Kelly. The dispatch was addressed to General Pemberton, at Jackson, Miss., stating that the Yankees had advanced to Pearl River, but finding that the ferry was destroyed, and that they could not cross, had left, taking a northeast course. The scouts had no difficulty in reaching the station, found the telegraph office, the operator and six or eight Confederate officers and soldiers standing and seated around, not having the least idea that any Yankees were on the south side of Pearl River.

The dispatch was examined and various questions asked by the parties, all of which were satisfactorily answered. The dispatch being sent the men complained of being hungry, and said they would cross over to the hotel, and mounting their horses they were half way over when up rode, in great haste, Mr. Sheriff number two, who had escaped the night before. He at once recognized the scouts as two of the party who had helped to drink his whiskey; the men knew him, too, and began to feel for their revolvers, while the sheriff, with naked sword in one hand and horse-pistol in the other—which proved to be empty—began to assume rather a dangerous character; at the same time shouting for help, and ordering everybody to stop them d——d Yankees. The men thought it would not pay to resist, so they prudently commenced a retreat.

Several persons tried to stop their horses, but the sharp crack of a revolver impressed them with the idea that it would not be a safe business, and gave them a wide berth. They met me within one mile of town. After stating their adventures I immediately sent one man back to report to the colonel, also to tell the advance guard to come on double quick, while with the remainder of my men we charged back into town, the rain at the time pouring down in torrents. The first place to visit was the depot. Not a soul was there except two old men; the rest had all absconded, the operator tearing up his instrument and taking it with him. He had not countermanded the dispatch, as was ascertained. When the two scouts retreated the Confederates thought that the Yankees were then in sight, and without waiting to secure their private property skedaddled, the honest sheriff with them.

Upon inquiry we learned that a train was soon due from the north. The usual precaution was taken to secure it; but after waiting half an hour beyond the time for its arrival the command became careless, and no further attention was given it, supposing that news had reached the next station of our approach. This was a sad mistake, for when everyone was scattered around town, thinking of anything else, the train came around the corner, from which point the engineer had a good view of a score of "blue coats." He "smelt a rat," and reversing his engine retreated safely with seventeen commissioned officers and eight millions in Confederate money, which was *en route* to pay off troops in Louisiana and Texas. A large lot of empty and loaded freight cars was burned, considerable commissary stores, four car-loads of ammunition, the telegraph cut in several places, the track torn up and some trestle-work destroyed.

The depot was spared on account of its being so near private buildings; they would undoubtedly have caught fire. This was a humane act, and was highly appreciated by the citizens. Though every precaution was taken by the officers to prevent the destruction of private property, the flames were soon seen to burst forth from a drug-store on the east side of the depot, resulting in the burning of three other buildings, two of which were empty stores and the third a private residence; none of the buildings were of very large dimensions. Every exertion was made to extinguish the fire and prevent its spreading.

Hazelhurst is in Copiah County, and is not a very large place; the buildings are somewhat scattered. But little taste or neatness is displayed, though we found some very clever people there, and some who still entertained a strong feeling for the old Union, and were bitterly opposed to secessionism. Two or three barrels of eggs and a quantity of sugar, flour and hams was found in the depot, which was taken to the hotel and cooked for all hands as long as it lasted.

The explosion of boxes of ammunition and bursting of some shells not only alarmed the citizens to some extent, but had a startling effect on Colonel Grierson and the column with him, which was about half way between the station and ferry. The order was given at once to "trot," then "gallop, march !" and they came charging into town, expecting to find Colonel Prince hotly engaged with the enemy. It was only the explosion of the ammunition and shells, that we had purposely fired, and they were sold again, as at Newton Station.

Captain Forbes, who was sent to Macon, rejoined the command just as the rear guard was crossing Pearl River. After the whole command reached Hazelhurst they rested four or five hours, giving me a good opportunity to listen to Captain Forbes relating his adventures, which I give as near as possible. On his way to Macon he was preceded by two of his scouts, Isaac E. Robinson and Wm. Buffington, both members of his own company. When within three miles of Macon they concluded to camp. Before reaching this place the scouts had captured twelve Confederate soldiers, picking them up one, two and three at a time.

While selecting the camp-ground Robinson was ordered to advance toward Macon about a mile, to see what he could learn about the force at that place. When he had gone about that distance, and dismounted, he heard the tramp of horses, and in a few minutes there approached him a squad of six Confederate soldiers. When within fifty yards he halted them, and demanded, "Who comes there?"

The answer came, "Friends."

The scout then said, "Advance one and give the countersign," whereupon one of them advanced, a captain, and the following conversation took place:

"You appear to be a picket here?"

"Yes, sir; have you not heard the 'Yanks' are coming?"

"Yes; I have learned that they are about six miles from here. I was not aware of any pickets stationed here."

"Oh, yes; I was sent here, and told to watch these cross-roads," (which were between him and the camp.)

"How many men are there of you?"

"Only about sixteen of us."

"What are your instructions about passing, &c?"

"The orders from General Loring (commanding forces then at Macon) are not to pass any soldiers, except commanding officers, and citizens."

"Well, my friend, I am a commanding officer, and have permission to take a squad of men and scout around the country."

"I will call the sergeant of the guard." He shouted at the top of his voice two or three times "sergeant of the guard," but no answer. By this time the soldiers began to be suspicious that all was not right, and two of them dropped back, soon followed by two more, leaving but one, who turned round and wanted to know "what in h—l they meant by leaving in that manner." They did not seem to pay any attention to him, but were soon on a gallop.

"Why, captain, you must have queer men, to leave in that way; I would not give much for such men to look after 'Yanks.'"

"I'll know what this means," he replied, and calling the fifth man, who still remained at his post, ordered him to remain there, and he would bring back the rascals, and away he went.

Robinson thought this was his opportunity, and he would improve it. The Confederate sat on his horse, with his double-barrelled gun elevated, cocked and ready for instant use. Robinson had on a long grey coat, beneath which his carbine hung, attached to a string; he slid his hand down beneath his coat, seizing his carbine and cocking it silently, unbuttoned his coat, and in an instant had it presented at the rebel's heart ordering him to drop his gun, ride forward and dismount, which he did. Robinson draws his revolver, drops his carbine, breaks the shot-gun, mounts his horse; ordering the reb to follow suit, hurries him back to Captain Forbes, who made the fellow believe that he would hang him if he did not tell all that he knew about the forces in Macon. The man had not been long in the service, was young and easily frightened, and informed the captain that there was about four hundred troops, mostly conscripts, stationed there, but there had arrived that day nine hundred troops from Mobile.

This was the same man captured by Federal forces as reported by Captain Lynch on his return from scout previously mentioned. Captain Forbes concluded not to visit Macon, and early next morning started back. After marching eight miles the scouts picked up a soldier belonging to the Second Mississippi Artillery. He happened to be one of those individuals that had been opposed to the war, but rather than be conscripted had volunteered. This man proved of considerable service to the captain, he having a good knowledge of the country; just the man the captain wanted, and he used him to good advantage. Striking towards the railroad, with the intention of cutting the telegraph and burning a bridge between Macon and Enterprise, to prevent a force being sent from the former to the latter place; but on nearing the railroad he learned that the bridge was strongly guarded; he concluded to avoid it, and destroying the telegraph proceeded towards Newton Station, at which place he was informed that Colonel Grierson had gone to Enterprise.

The captain had a tedious time reaching this point, having to go through swamps, swim streams, travel through timber without any roads, for hours at a time, in order to avoid forces that were patrolling the country in quest of us. From Newton Station he went the nearest route to Enterprise, and when within one mile of the town learned that a force of three thousand rebel troops were just getting off the cars. He promptly raised a white flag and rode forward, demanding the surrender of the town in the name of Colonel Grierson! To this demand the rebel commander, Colonel Goodwin, asked an hour to consider upon it, and inquired of the captain where he would be found at the end of that time. Captain Forbes replied that he would fall back to the reserve.

It is not known whether Enterprise surrendered or not, although an article was read in the *Jackson-Granada-Memphis-Appeal,* of April 26th, that fifteen hundred "Yanks" had demanded the surrender of the place. The captain made good use of the hour in getting to the reserve. He followed our trail for four days, making forced marches of sixty miles a day, swimming streams, over which we had burned the bridges, to prevent the enemy following us. At one time they were taken in a windfall purposely by a guide, with the intention of having them captured, but their scheme was discovered in time to avoid it. Previous to this, and near Philadelphia, one of the scouts was shot dead from an ambush, (William Buffington,) also a member of the company wounded, (C. E. Martin,) both good and brave soldiers.

When near Raleigh, Robinson learned that a company of guerrillas were in that place. The captain ordered a charge, and so complete was the surprise (they thinking that all the "Yanks" had passed) that not one of them escaped. They were taking dinner, and ere they knew it, they were surrounded; they numbered twenty-nine men. Their arms were destroyed, men turned loose, the horses and captain of the company taken along. After leaving this place, Lieut. McCausland suggested to Captain Forbes that if he would let him he would send three men, well mounted, to overtake Colonel Grierson. His request was granted, and I have previously mentioned how successful they were. Captain Forbes and men deserve great praise for their bravery and perseverance. He was highly complimented by Colonel Grierson for his success.

At seven o'clock the command left Hazelhurst, the Sixth Illinois in advance. Taking a northwest course it proceeded towards Galiton. It now became necessary to use every precaution. We had passed within twenty-five miles of the capital of the State—cut the railroad and telegraph communications on the New Orleans and Great Northern Railroad. The enemy's scouts had been sent out, and were watching our movements; couriers were flying in every direction, spreading the news, forces were concentrating and sent to intercept us, hem us in and annihilate us, as they boasted, and felt confident of accomplishing. They certainly had every advantage on their side;—a perfect knowledge of the country—every road, public or private—every stream of water, small or large—the fordable places and bridges—forces above and below us on the railroad, in our front at Port Gibson, Grand Gulf and Port Hudson—following in our rear—retreat was impossible, even if such an idea had occurred to us, we having destroyed our only hope in that quarter—bridges and ferries.

Colonel Grierson was not one of the retreating kind; his motto was "*onward.*" In wood craft I do not think I ever saw his equal. He reminded me of an old deer hunter; he understood the runways and the shortest way to get to them; besides he had good supporters in the following persons: Colonel Prince and Lieut.-Col. Blackburn, of the

Seventh Illinois; Lieut.-Col. Loomis and Adj't. S. L. Woodward, of the Sixth Illinois. It was seldom that any citizen was found to act as guide, except when dodging across through the woods from one road to another. With one of Colton's maps—a small pocket companion—with the states and counties on it, he made his way through the enemy's country. The road selected, it was then the duty of the scouts to keep its communication open, thereby causing no delay to the column.

Colonel Grierson was, just at this time, executing one of his flank movements, which had so many times thrown the enemy off our track, leaving them far in our rear. It was about nine o'clock when we entered the small town of Galiton, driving out a few guerrillas. We had not proceeded many miles further when a train of wagons was discovered ahead, drawn by oxen. The scouts were withdrawn; the Sixth Illinois dashed ahead, and after a few shots fired, captured a thirty-two pound Parrott gun, fourteen hundred pounds of powder, two wagons, and some provisions, *en route* for Grand Gulf.

The gun was spiked, wagon and powder destroyed. After proceeding a few miles further, we went into camp at Hargrove's. Distance travelled, thirty-seven miles.

It was very amusing, sometimes, to witness the astonishment depicted on the countenances of the negroes when they learned that we were Yankees. So many falsehoods had been told them by their masters and mistresses that we were a different people—ugly, deformed, and very wicked, that the poor slaves had conjured up in their minds a fearful picture; they being naturally superstitious and ignorant, are easily worked upon. I had stopped one day to feed at a large plantation, and was somewhat surprised at not seeing any negroes about; however the mystery was soon solved, by finding an old negro in one of the cabins, whose aged locks of wool had turned "gray." I asked him where all the negroes were.

"I tell you, massa, dey am in de woods; you see I'se an old nigger, but I knows better, massa; I tell dem not to run to de wood to hide, de Lord knows I did; yes, massa, dey am in de woods over dar,"—pointing with his hand. I asked him why they had run away; we would not harm them. "Well, I tells you, massa; de white folks tell we black ones dat you all's will kill us; so dey hear dat the "Yank's" be coming, and dey runs; now, massa, Ise like to ax one question."

"Well, Uncle, go ahead."

"I wish you tells dis old nigger when am all de black folks to be free."

Smilingly I replied, "just as soon as Uncle Abraham sounds his trumpet, so that it will be heard throughout the whole land, then he will fold you all in his bosom, and you will become a free and happy people."

I left the old darkey repeating to himself, "De Lord send him this way soon!" Upon reaching the yard I found that some of the men had flanked around into the woods, looking for horses, and discovered the negroes hid behind stumps and logs. They thought their time had come, and exhibited much fear, which was soon quieted by the kind manner in which our men approached them. They became quite docile, and had a great curiosity to see the "horns" they had heard stuck out of our heads.

TWELFTH DAY.

After a good night's rest we left camp at seven o'clock. We had changed our course, and were going due south—the roads in good condition. Nothing occurred to interrupt us except now and then a chase, and frequently capturing one or two guerrillas, who were in our advance. Thus we continued until about ten o'clock, when the column was halted, and after a council of half an hour among the officers, the following companies of the Seventh Illinois were detached: A, H, F and M under command of Captain Trafton, (acting major) whose instructions were to proceed to Bahala, on the New Orleans and Great Northern Railroad, below Hazelhurst, to destroy the track and otherwise injure the enemy.

Colonel Blackburn ordered me to take one man and accompany this expedition. Away we went, taking a left-hand road, while the rest of the command moved forward on the road to Union Church, the Sixth Illinois in advance, which I will leave to resume their journey while I take my place in the advance with Stedman. Not meeting with anything until within one mile of Bahala, when on gaining the top of a hill (country thickly timbered), I was somewhat startled, at first, to discover two army tents not more than seventy-five yards distant. I immediately halted, cautioned my command to be silent; taking a hasty survey, could not see a living being. We then retreated and reported to Captain Trafton; the column was halted, we concluded there was either no person with the tents, or they knew of our approach and were ready to ambush us.

The captain at once decided to advance, by deploying one company as skirmishers, and throwing one company on the right and left flank, the fourth bringing up the centre, moving up cautiously, each moment expecting to hear the sharp crack of the rifle. The skirmishers are within a few yards of the tents, still no signs of life; the tents are surrounded, they are captured, they are ours; contents—one darkey asleep; loss—none. It appears that a squad of cavalry had been camped here, and were engaged in burning coal for the Confederate Government, and had been withdrawn the day previous, being ordered to Osako. The negro had been left to take care of the tents, which were destroyed, together with a large quantity of coal. I was then ordered to proceed forward and reconnoitre the town.

I did so by flanking around through the timber. Could see no signs of any force there—all appeared to be quiet. Reported back to the command, which went in on a charge, capturing a Major Weader, belonging on General Gardner's staff, and was chief commissary of subsistence, and very much of a gentleman. After destroying depot, water-tank, tressle-work, and steam-engine for pumping water and sawing wood, we rested a short time and then began retracing our steps, taking the major along. After travelling about seven miles we stopped at a plantation and fed, then continued our journey. On coming into the main road upon which we were to follow up Colonel Grierson, it was eight o'clock, and we had thirty miles to travel before reaching the command.

After proceeding about a mile I stopped at a plantation, and what was my surprise to learn that a force of the enemy had passed about five hours before, and were following up Colonel Grierson, but were in ignorance of any Federal force sent to Bahala. They were under the impression that all the Yankee forces had passed. This was most fortunate for us, and in another respect we were favoured—the night was very dark. I immediately reported to Captain Trafton. The men were all ordered to observe silence, arrangements were perfected so that the column should halt whenever the scouts requested it, and all seemed to depend on them for a safe reunion with the command. Only Stedman and myself were acting as scouts.

Half a mile further I saw a candle-light, apparently out of doors. I advanced boldly, and when near enough discovered an old man standing out upon the front stoop of the house, holding the light in one hand and shading his eyes with the other. He appeared to be conversing with a man that was mounted on a horse, and inside of the garden lot. As I drew up to the gate, not more than fifty yards from the house, I cried out "Hello, step this way;" this seemed to come unexpectedly, and in a moment the mounted man disappeared in the darkness. The old gentleman wanted to know who was there.

"A friend," I replied; "please step this way a moment, I want to ask you some questions."

He toddled out to the gate, and as soon as he could see asked if I was not a soldier. I answered that I was, and wished to know how long since our troops passed.

"Do you mean Colonel Adams, sir?"

"Yes, and what force has he?"

"Well, I don't know as I can tell; I can't see but a short distance, but there appeared to be a good many pass, then some cannon."

"How long since?" I inquired.

"Well, about five hours, or it may be six."

"Who was that man that was talking with you when I came up?"

"Well, I really don't know; he is a soldier and a stranger to me, and was inquiring the way to Port Hudson."

"Well, goodnight, we must go, for we have got reinforcements for Colonel Adams. Tell that man, if you see him, not to be alarmed, the Yankees are all ahead, and we expect to overtake them tomorrow."

"I hope you will," said the old man, "they took two horses and a mule from me, and my neighbour down here lost three mules and one horse, besides four of his best working hands."

I turned and left him, thinking the horse and mule business was nothing new to me. I had no sooner returned to the head of the column and reported to Captain Trafton, then up came a single horseman. It at once occurred to me that this was the man talking with the old man at the house. I told the men to keep still, at the same time ordering him to halt, which he obeyed promptly, and in a loud voice said, "I am all right, I belong to the Confederate army; I heard you talk with the man at the house." Captain Trafton then told him to advance; coming up rapidly he displayed a double-barrelled gun laying across the pommel of his saddle. I asked him if he was not tired, at the same time requesting him to hand me his gun and I would have one of the men carry it for him; he handed it over and I passed it back.

Just then Captain Trafton says to me, "This man may be a Yankee for all we know."

"Oh, no, gentlemen, you are mistaken; I am a lieutenant, and belong to Port Hudson, and can tell you all about it, and who commands there, then captain you can tell if I ain't all right."

He was rather young, had been on furlough, and was now on his way back to join his company. He said we would find six men stopping at the next plantation, patrols and pickets, belonging to Wirt Adams' Louisiana cavalry—just what we wanted to know. He was allowed to ride in the ranks, upon being persuaded to accompany us. The men all understood the game, and the lieutenant proved very sociable, little dreaming that he was a prisoner.

After travelling another mile I met a mounted soldier, with a small boy behind him, passed them back as prisoners and continued on until reaching a plantation—a barn on the left of the road, the house on the right; from the barn to the house was about three hundred yards. Approaching the barn we found three men feeding their horses, which they had unsaddled, their saddles laying on the ground; two shot-guns and one carbine standing against the fence next the road. They heard us coming up. I stopped at the gate; they appeared to be expecting us, and expressed no surprise—entered into conversation; questions were asked on both sides and satisfactorily answered. I then told Stedman—in an undertone—to go back and tell the captain to send a few men forward, and as Stedman started I spoke loud, telling him to tell the captain that all was right, that we would soon join Colonel Adams.

In a few minutes the men came up, and without further parley we took them prisoners, which proceeding somewhat surprised them. They had stated that three of their number were at the house, and as some loud talking had been done, might they not have heard it? An idea occurred to me, which I at once put into execution. Telling four or five men to come with me, I galloped up to the house, and speaking in a loud voice said, "Come along, men; you know what the captain's orders are, that we must find and bring along every man that is straggling behind; every man is needed to whip those d——d Yankees."

This had the desired effect. They were in the house one a lieutenant having a good time conversing with the ladies. Skulking was beneath their dignity, and as they heard what I said came boldly out. The men had dismounted, and slipping through the gate took the gentlemen by surprise. Their arms were secured and they put under guard. The Port Hudson lieutenant for the first time "smelt a rat," and exclaimed, "D—n me, if I ain't sold!"

A sad accident occurred at this place. Several shot-guns were found; I had destroyed all but one, a very fine double-barrelled shot-gun, which Sergeant G. M. Vaughn, company F, took a fancy to, requesting me not to break it, but give it to him, and he would carry it. I handed it to him, at the same time saying that he would soon get tired of it,

51

which proved to be the case sooner than I anticipated. We were just going to start when we were startled by the report of firearms. The sergeant had concluded not to keep the gun, and dismounting went a few steps to a tree, and grasping the barrel in both hands near the muzzle raised it up, striking it against the tree. He had not taken the necessary precaution to remove the caps, and the result was he lodged the contents of one barrel of buck-shot in his thigh. He had to be left, and I never expected to see him again. The inmates of the house promised to show him every kindness. We resumed our journey, and while passing a cross-road five rebels came trotting into our column, thinking we were Confederates. They were taken quietly, without firing a shot. A short time after this occurred two patrols were met and secured.

It was now about midnight, when on consulting with the captain he thought it was advisable to know something more about the force between us and Colonel Grierson, as well as the locality of the country, and see that, if necessary, we could not flank around the enemy and join our command. We were then within sight of a large plantation. It was a dim starlight night, and the country through which we were travelling principally timbered, with tolerable good roads. The column halted, and taking two men we jumped over a fence, crossed an open space about two hundred yards and stopped in front of a neat log house. I then stationed one man on each side, to prevent anyone from leaving it, and then stepping upon the verandah knocked loudly at the door.

A voice from within inquired, "Who's there?"

I answered, "A soldier; my captain has sent me here to find out something about the roads, and how long since Colonel Adams passed; we are trying to overtake Colonel Adams with reinforcements."

By this time he told me to come in. The door not being locked I turned the knob and stepped into a small-sized room, containing one bed, a few chairs, a table, a looking-glass, and a fireplace in which were a few burning embers, giving sufficient light to see that the room was but scantily furnished. He requested me to light a candle and then be seated, which I soon accomplished, while he remained in bed. The following conversation then took place. He was a lawyer and a bachelor, living at his ease, owning considerable property, and did not appear to have seen more than thirty-five years, very good looking, with penetrating eyes, rather prepossessing countenance, and no doubt prided himself on his cuteness as a lawyer.

52

"Well, you say you are a soldier, and that your captain has sent you here to obtain information about Colonel Adams and the condition of the roads. Now, sir, before answering your questions, I will ask you a few. To whose command do you belong?"

"To Colonel Faulkner's First Mississippi Cavalry, stationed at Granada, and sent by railroad to Jackson, to assist in intercepting the Yankees at Pearl River, but we arrived too late; the Yankees had crossed, and we were ordered by a dispatch from General Pemberton to pursue the enemy, and, if possible, fall in with Colonel Adams and report to him."

"Is Colonel Faulkner in command of this force."

"No, sir; Major Williams is in command. We number about two hundred men, well armed and uniformed. Having been engaged in several battles with the enemy, most of the men have captured Yankee clothing sufficient to clothe themselves."

"You do not speak like a Southern man."

"That is easily accounted for; I came from Missouri formerly; belonged to Jeff. Thompson's command; when he disbanded I came to West Tennessee and joined this command. But I must not delay; can you send a negro along to guide us through to Union Church?"

"I have several blacks, but my horses and mules I sent away when I received news that the Yankees were coming this way, in order to save them. I would go myself as your guide if I had my riding horse here, for I am acquainted with Colonel Adams, and it will be a capital idea, this reinforcement; yes, I would like to go—the colonel stopped here half an hour and rested his column."

"Do you know, sir, how much force Colonel Adams had?"

"About four hundred men, with six pieces of artillery. He left here about sundown, and intended to attack the Yankees at three o'clock in their rear, while a force from Port Hudson will meet them in front, on the Natchez road."

"I would like very much you would accompany us; I can mount you on a good horse."

"I will go;" and suiting his action to his word sprang out of bed and commenced dressing, saying that he would be ready in five minutes, and that I would find a saddle, bridle and sheepskin on the doorsteps."

"What may I call your name, sir?"

"My name is Mosby."

"Well, Mr. Mosby, I will step out and tell the major, and have a horse brought up for you." So out I went, feeling very much relieved; told the captain all about my conversation and my representations of the command, also the information I had obtained, thoroughly posting the captain. I then had the horse brought forward, and the two men withdrawn from the house, the captain in the meantime procuring a long grey coat and cap of the same colour.

All was now ready, and Mr. Mosby made his appearance at the fence, jumped over, and I introduced them. The captain occupying the advance the lawyer had no opportunity of seeing the column. I proceeded to the front, leaving the captain and lawyer riding side by side, on intimate terms. We were now within twelve miles of Union Church, and it was of the utmost importance that Colonel Grierson should be informed, at all hazards, of the designs of the enemy. I had gone about two miles when I met two patrols; unarmed them, turning them out on one side of the road, in order that Mr. Mosby should not see them near enough to recognize their features or dress.

As we continued to move on, tired and hungry, I thought someone might try and reach Colonel Grierson before three o'clock; I dropped back so as to ride in company with Mr. Mosby, and inquired of him, where he thought Colonel Adams would stop to feed and prepare before making the attack, and if it was a possible thing for any person to get around his camp without being discovered, as my design was to reach as near the "Yanks" as possible and find out their position, which would be a great advantage to us. Mr. Mosby thought Colonel Adams would feed near the Fayette road on a plantation; that it was impossible to get around Colonel Adams' camp and return in time, owing to the rugged state of the country; "But," continued he, "I am well acquainted with Colonel Adams, and I will go with you, and can pass you through his lines, then you can have a good road to proceed on."

I then inquired how far it was to where the colonel would camp, Mr. Mosby replied about four miles. It was near one o'clock, p.m. I told Mr. Mosby I would consider his proposition, and if I concluded to go through Colonel Adams' camp I would return for him. I started ahead, accompanied by Stedman. We had now made up our minds to go ahead and see if we could obtain a view of the rebel camp, and if possible reach Colonel Grierson.

I bid some of my comrades goodbye, telling them that I did not know whether ever I would see them again or not. We started alone; the road was shaded—the overhanging trees on either side, which, together with the darkness of the night, made it very lonely. I began to reflect; what, if we should be detected, our fate was certain death—we would be treated as spies. Then imagination pictured home with all its inducements, and I could see many sad countenances and bitter tears. I thought of all this; what if we should be successful in the attempt, might we not be the instrument of saving the lives of many brave comrades, (we said we would go, and go we must,) and I prayed in my heart that God would guide us safely through.

We had advanced to within one half mile of the supposed camp ground, when I could distinctly hear somebody talking and laughing; we came to a halt, and when near enough I could see the figures of the men mounted upon horses; I allowed them to come within about twenty-five yards, when I cried halt, which sound came rather unexpected to them, and at first they did not know whither to turn and run or not, but raising their guns I could distinctly hear the sharp click of the hammers as they cocked their pieces. Our revolvers were grasped in our right hands ready for instant use. (a precaution we always used after night.) I immediately inquired "who comes there?" One of them answered, "friends," I then said, "advance one and give the countersign."

They answered they had no countersign, at the same time one of them advanced, and as he came up, inquired who I was, and if I was alone. By this time I could see my man plain enough to feel satisfied that he was a Confederate soldier. I answered him that I was not alone, that the column would be here in a few minutes, that we had been travelling all day and that night to overtake Colonel Adams and reinforce him; "all right," says he, "we belong to old Wirt Adams' cavalry, and tomorrow we intend to give the 'Yanks' h—l." By this time the other two came up and many questions were asked as to the command we belonged to, all of which we answered satisfactorily. They informed me that the "Yanks" had a fight going into Union Church last evening, and that Colonel Adams had gone to Fayette there to be reinforced by troops from the river, and they intended to ambush the "Yanks" in the morning between Fayette and Union Church; that the "Yanks" intended to make Natches but would get where the Fayette road turned off to notify forces coming up where they could join Colonel Adams.

This was just what I wanted to know and I felt really good. I knew the column would soon be along, and telling my friends that I would go back and meet the advance, and tell them of their presence, so that no accident would occur. This looked plausible enough, and without

55

any objections they permitted me to depart. I then procured two men from one of the company's, proceeded ahead, and without any trouble took my three friends in "out of the wet"—two of them were lieutenants, they had left their post and were going to a plantation about a mile from there to visit an old acquaintance. They were taken a few yards into the timber to prevent Mr. Mosby seeing them, fearing that he would know them. As soon as the head of the column had passed the prisoners were turned over to company M. I started forward and as I passed Mr. Mosby he inquired who those men were that we had taken; I told him they were "Yanks" and had been straggling from their command, probably to plunder, and had lost their way. He allowed it was a capital idea, and hoped we would shoot them, that they should not be permitted to live.

The coast was now clear, and we had only six miles to go before joining our command. I now told Mr. Mosby that Colonel Adams had gone to Fayette, and explained the reason. Mr. Mosby then wanted to know from the major whether he intended joining Colonel Adams or following up the "Yanks." The major (which we will continue to call Captain Trafton,) replied, that on considering the matter he would follow the "Yanks" and send a courier through to Colonel Adams, notifying him of the force here and the intention, which was to attack the enemy in the rear, in conjunction with their attack in the front.

Mr. Mosby thought it was a capital idea and offered his services to carry this dispatch through to Colonel Adams—in fact insisted upon it. But the major allowed that he could not part so easily with his excellent company, and turning to me, ordered me to send a courier through to Colonel Adams on the Fayette road which we were now leaving to our right; I absented myself a short time, then reported to the major that his order was obeyed. I then trotted forward beside my friend Stedman and we congratulated each other on the success attending us, and it was not without a feeling of gratitude to the Most High for our safety thus far.

We now felt comparatively safe. It was but five miles to the command, and I gave myself up to thoughts of our numerous adventures, of the past few hours, and could hardly realise that we had had so many narrow escapes; I thought of the delay I had occasioned the column so many times, knowing how tired and sleepy the men were, how they must have cursed me, but they were ignorant of the proceeding in front, and as the prisoners continued to be sent back they began to realise the importance of the scouts, and their show of gratitude toward myself and comrade afterward has more than repaid me for the risk incurred.

When within a few miles of Union Church I could see our picket fires, so riding briskly up, though not without being halted by the vidette. I advised the men of our having a guide who was under the impression that he was rendering the Confederate service a great benefit by guiding us. I requested them not to make any remark while the head of the column was passing, that would excite suspicion in the mind of Mosby. I dropped back to see what effect the presence of this picket post would have on him; at first, he was much surprised and remarked that he did not know that we had any force ahead. I told him that it was only one company, that had been sent down on the east side of the railroad, and were waiting here expecting us—that we still had a force at Union Church. This was satisfactory; he allowed it was a capital idea.

We soon entered the town, and with it came daylight—half-past four o'clock. We found the command scattered, and laying stretched out on the ground fast asleep—for the weather was quite warm and pleasant. We at once dismounted, the men feeding their horses, while Captain Trafton—no longer major—repaired to headquarters and communicated his information to Colonel Grierson. The prisoners were put under guard, except Mr. Mosby, who remained most of the time in my company, and not suspecting anything wrong. Colonel Grierson at once arose from his bed and sent for Colonel Prince, Lieut.-Col. Blackburn, Lieut.-Col. Loomis, and Adj't S. L. Woodward; the latter he consulted on all such occasions.

After Captain Trafton left on his expedition to Bahala, the rest of the command kept on the direct road to Union Church, not meeting with any trouble until within two miles of the place, except eight or ten guerrillas, who were picked up by the scouts. Companies A, C, and D, the advance of the Sixth Illinois, met the enemy about one hundred and fifty strong, but without any delay drove them into and through town some three miles, wounding two and taking several prisoners. Our loss one—slightly wounded. Captain Trafton brought in twenty-one prisoners, having met with no loss, except the accident, and having travelled about thirty miles more than the rest of the command. While Colonel Grierson was consulting the map, Adj't Root was busily engaged writing paroles, and soon the prisoners were brought up to sign their names.

This was what I wanted; now was the time to witness the surprise and discomfiture of our worthy friend, Mr. Mosby, the learned lawyer, the Yankee exterminator, "a capital idea." As the prisoners were brought around to the front of the house, and going through the ceremony of being paroled, my friend the lawyer's curiosity was excited; he thought he recognized among the prisoners a few familiar faces, and expressed a desire to cross the garden and see.

"Most certainly," I replied, "there's no objection to any one conversing with the prisoners." He started, and I remained standing where I could see and watch his countenance. On the verandah was a table, and seated around it the busy clerks, while the prisoners crowded around, awaiting their turn to be called, apparently feeling in good spirits. On approaching the crowd one of them turned around and at once recognized, in the form and features of Mr. Mosby, an old acquaintance, and extending his hand exclaimed, "Why, friend Mosby, you here; I did not expect to see you a prisoner."

"Why, explain; what do you mean? are these not our troops?"

"Our troops? No! I wish they were; I'd feel a d——d sight better than I do now. No, sir; they are the genuine Yankees; but they will not do anything with you, being a citizen, and not a soldier; but I am surprised, lawyer Mosby, that you had not noticed the difference."

I could see his face change colour—half a dozen times—and turning around he looked "daggers" at me. In a few minutes he returned, and looking me full in the face said, "This is a d——d Yankee trick."

I was full of laughter, and laying my hand familiarly on his shoulder said, "Mr. Mosby, you are sold, but it is all fair in war times, and do you not think 'a capital idea?'" He twitched his mouth a little, and at last assuming a contented look said, "Sergeant, you have done well, but for God's sake do not ever mention this to any person." I promised, but it was too good to keep. From that time until he left the place he was very sociable. On inquiring how he was to get back home, he said he could not walk so far, and there would not be a horse or mule left. I told him that I thought I could raise him a horse of some kind, as several had to be left behind.

I left him, and finding the colonel, asked him if there would be any horses left behind, if so, I would like one for Mr. Mosby to return on. The colonel told me to find one and mount him. I soon found one, and putting on a good saddle called Mr. Mosby, and handing him the reins told him to keep this horse in remembrance of the Yankees. He seemed much pleased, and when I left him he had a very favourable opinion of Yankee hospitality. Prisoners all paroled, exhausted horses turned loose, by six o'clock in the morning we left Union Church.

THIRTEENTH DAY.

The twenty-ninth found us directing our course towards the railroad—the Seventh Illinois in advance—passing through the woods for several miles without any signs of a road—another flank movement—leaving Colonel Adams with a considerable force on the Natchez road, expecting to ambush us. We afterwards learned that he did not discover we had evacuated Union Church until two o'clock that day.

We were now directing our course towards Brookhaven, on the New Orleans and Great Northern railroad. Considerable dodging was done the first three or four hours' march of this day. I do not think we missed travelling toward any point of the compass. We were making tolerably fast time, occasionally "taking in" a prisoner. Finally we struck the main road leading to Brookhaven, and met ox and mule teams drawing hogsheads of sugar, running it off from the station across the country to Port Gibson; of course it. was destroyed, but not before the men replenished their haversacks. When within four miles of the station we surprised and took prisoners five guerrillas, without firing a shot. Upon searching a house nearby we found eight shotguns and rifles, and three revolvers.

Destroying the former we advanced to within two miles of the station, when I was ordered to proceed and reconnoitre the town, and see what I could discover. About one mile from town I met a squad of eight soldiers walking; they had no arms and were on their way to join their command at Port Hudson. I sent one man back with them to the column. Coming within sight of the town I could see a considerable number of men collected here and there on the corners of the streets, but could not see any armed soldiers. I reported back to the column, which advanced, and as soon as in sight, and not more than four hundred yards from town, a single shot was heard to our left, in the timber.

This place being entirely surrounded by woods, the column formed fours, and on a charge dashed into town through the streets, causing some confusion, excitement, and a considerable running among the citizens; they anticipated a visit from the "Yanks," but not so soon. The shot was a signal of our approach, but ere the echo of the report died away we were in and among them. While the Seventh was charging in this gallant style, the Sixth was making good time towards a camp of instruction, one and a half miles south of town, which they charged

59

into, expecting to find a considerable force, principally conscripts; but they had left the evening previous—some eight hundred. This camp was capable of accommodating about fifteen thousand troops. Long rows of small frame buildings, a few tents, a quantity of arms, and a large supply of commissary stores were destroyed. It was truly a most delightful camping-ground, situated on a high hill, in a shady grove of live oaks.

Captain Lynch, of the Sixth Illinois, with companies E and F, was sent to destroy one mile of trestle-work. After accomplishing this work, the Sixth visited town, in time to see the flames devouring the depot and some dozen freight cars, fired by the Seventh; also a railroad bridge. The depot contained quite a quantity of commissary stores.

Two hundred and sixteen prisoners were captured and paroled here, principally sick and convalescent soldiers. They were quartered in a very fine building, used as a hospital; they seemed to court our society rather than avoid it, and evinced a strong desire to be paroled, which was a long, tedious task, they having to be written out, which duty devolved on Adjutants Root and Woodward, both young men possessing a large share of patience and perseverance. Several citizens were hiding themselves in the woods, and as soon as they learned that we were not destroying private property came into town, and urgently requested that they be paroled, so as to avoid the conscription. In the meantime somebody was enjoying a good meal. Lieut.-Col. Blackburn had ordered at one of the hotels dinner for two hundred of his men, paying the proprietor in Confederate money. The landlord expressed a wish that the "Yanks" would come every day, if they all acted like "we'uns" did.

When the depot was burning there was great danger of a private building taking fire on the opposite side of the street, owing to the excessive heat thrown upon it; and had it not been for the exertions of some twenty soldiers, who brought pails of water and kept the roof wet, it would have burned and destroyed many more with it. The saving of the property was personally superintended by Colonel Grierson.

I must say that the citizens of this town were generally very clever, opening their doors and inviting us to partake of their hospitality; there was none of that bitterness and hatred displayed. They were mostly of an educated class, whose minds had not been prejudiced by the extravagant tales circulated through the South concerning us. A show of neatness and taste prevailed around these dwellings. Brookhaven has a very pretty location. It is in Lawrence County, and has a population of about fifteen hundred. It was near sundown when we took our departure, leaving the people enjoying a much better opinion of us than they had before. From this place we marched six miles and camped, and for the first time in thirty-eight hours did a portion of the command take the saddles off their horses, and obtain time to sleep.

FOURTEENTH DAY.

The command moved out just at sunrise, with every appearance of a lovely day—the Sixth Illinois in the advance. Without any interruption we proceeded to Boyachitta, a small station on the railroad, consisting of not more than a dozen houses. While the Sixth Illinois was destroying the depot and six or eight freight cars, Captain Hening, of the Seventh, with his company, was sent to destroy some trestle-work and a railroad bridge. Upon reaching them he found it to be a bigger job than he could complete in the short space of time allowed on such occasions, so the captain sent back to the Lieut.-Col. of the Sixth Illinois to send fifty or one hundred men to assist in destroying the very large railroad bridge and two hundred and fifty feet of trestle-work—a very important item. Captain Lynch, of the Sixth Illinois, with company E, destroyed three hundred feet of trestle-work. From here we proceeded towards Summit, crossing the railroad to the east between the former and latter place, destroying railroad bridges and trestle-work as we went along. Two couriers were captured by the scouts. We arrived in Summit about noon; marched in quietly and leisurely.

The people seemed to expect us, and there were no signs of excitement or fear displayed, either in actions or features. They had received a favourable report of our conduct at Brookhaven, and Colonel Grierson was almost as much of a favourite with them as General Pemberton. We spent nearly half a day here, improving the time by destroying a large number of freight cars and a large quantity of sugar, salt, molasses and meal—government property—which was loaded into the cars and then run down the track, away from private property, and burned. The depot was spared from the flames because it would endanger dwellings.

Some of the men discovered that there were thirty or forty barrels of Louisiana rum hid in the swamp, about a mile from town—the meanest stuff in existence, warranted to kill further than any rifle in Uncle Sam's service. Some of the men began to feel quite uneasy, and the swamp became a place of much resort. The colonel soon heard of it, and sent a commissioned officer, with a squad of men, to destroy it; they with great reluctance stove in the head of each barrel, and thus did waste the balm of a thousand flowers. In justice to the citizens, I will say they knew what good liquor was, and kept it, too. You will ask, where? buried in a pile of old chips. Now, who but a Yankee would think of looking in a pile of old rubbish, in a dirty door-yard? A four-gallon demijohn was pulled out from its hiding-place, filled to the brim with good "old rye," such as would make a temperance man forget his pledge. Upon entering a house one day I heard the latter part of a conversation between a mother and daughter. The latter was in a mild way trying to convince her mother that it was no use trying to hide anything from the Yankees; "Aunty hid her wine out in the cornfield, and some of the nasty scamps found it."

Some of the men had a curiosity to see the inside of a large hall; the door being fastened they did not wish to break the lock, but took the trouble to find the proprietor, who, on learning the object of their visit, was very reluctant to comply with their request. He was informed that if he did not produce the keys they would break it down. This was enough; he handed over the keys and the men entered the hall, finding several old United States muskets, and folded neatly underneath them was a silk battle-flag, with a motto inscribed on it—"*God and our rights,*" "Fort Donelson," "Shiloh"—belonging to a Mississippi regiment—I have forgotten the number. The men of course confiscated it. At this place we found plenty of feed for our horses. The citizens were kind to us, and, like their neighbours at Brookhaven, showed many signs of loyalty toward the old Union. This place showed many signs of once having done considerable business; of a neat, lively appearance, a pretty location, situated in Pike County, and before the war could boast of a population of about three thousand.

Just as the sun was sinking to rest "boots and saddles "was sounded, and we left town amid smiles and the waving of many handkerchiefs, following a southwest course in the direction of Liberty. After travelling eight miles we camped for the night. After leaving Summit we passed through some fine country and over good roads. The climate was delightful. We were not more than one hundred miles from New Orleans. Were we going there? that was the question.

A rebel courier had been captured since leaving the railroad. The scouts had learned that there was a force at Osyko Station. There was now every indication that the enemy were exerting their utmost to intercept us. Large forces were reported in various directions—delay would prove fatal to us. Colonel Grierson concluded to abandon the railroad and take a straight line for Baton Rouge, Louisiana. We had completely destroyed forty miles of the road, and the command was becoming very weary for want of proper rest. So far as horses were concerned there was no scarcity; many troopers had to change four or five times, abandoning their worn out ones, and but few of the horses we started with were taken through; besides we were in poor trim for fighting, there being only forty rounds of ammunition to each man, and it was not the intention of Colonel Grierson to engage the enemy, but rather avoid him. I am satisfied of one thing—that had we been compelled to fight it would have been a desperate one. A better understanding and feeling never existed between two regiments than between these two so linked together. I will speak more of them hereafter.

Fifteenth Day.

On the morning of the first of May, just as daylight began to appear, the command left camp, taking a southwest course—Seventh Illinois in advance—and as we wended our way through the woodlands, we little dreamed what a change would be produced in a few hours. The sun arose in all his glory—not one cloud visible in the sky to obscure its dazzling brightness.

A gentle breeze floated through the trees, causing a rustling among the green leaves of the oaks. Perched among the branches was the mocking bird, singing a variety of notes, the whole impressing the beholder with a sense of a Creator of all this beauty. The command felt inspired, and various were the conjectures as to what point on the Mississippi River we would make. We were sometimes pursuing by-roads, and it was on one of these, and within four miles of the Clinton and Osyko road, that we met a sutler driving his team, seated in a wagon. Following him was a man mounted on a fine horse, from whom I obtained some information respecting their forces. They were on their way to Osyko, not expecting to meet, but rather avoid us, under the impression that we were advancing on another road. Among the stock was some tobacco, to which the men helped themselves.

About ten o'clock we emerged into the Clinton and Osyko road. I at once discovered, by the newly-made tracks, that a column had passed, and could not have been long before. Sending a man back to Colonel Grierson, he soon came up and examined closely. It was the opinion of all the officers that a considerable force had passed, and were going in the same direction as ourselves. I was then ordered by Colonel Grierson to advance cautiously, to let nothing escape my observation on either side of the road, and if I saw any object that I could not satisfy myself about, to report at once to him, and not to get more than half a mile from the advance.

After receiving these instructions I started, followed by my scouts; had proceeded about two and a half miles when I discovered horses hitched in the edge of the timber, near the roadside on our left; I could see that they were saddled, but could not discover any person around. We were then about three hundred yards from them. I immediately sent one man back to report to Colonel Grierson, and taking two of them with me started on, using the necessary precaution of having our revolvers ready at hand. As we approached nearer I could see that there were but three horses and three men, two of them sitting upon a log talking, the third lying down. They were well armed, each man carrying a carbine and revolver. They did not seem to think strange of our approach.

We rode up to them and I said, "Hello, boys, on picket?"

"Yes; been on about an hour and feel devilish tired; been travelling night and day after the d——d 'Yanks,' and I'll bet my horse they will get away yet."

"That is just our case," I replied; "but where is your command?"

"Over in the rush bottom, resting"—pointing with his hand.

"Whose command is it, and how many have you?"

Just then two shots were heard in our rear, and sounded as though fired on the right of the road. At this they began to open their eyes and prick up their ears. There was no time for further questioning, so giving the men the sign, each one of us covered his man with his revolver, demanding their surrender, and to hand over their arms at once or we would blow them through, and ordering them to mount, double-quicked them back to the column, which was halted some four hundred yards in our rear. In order that the reader may more fully understand the situation of affairs, I will try and describe the surrounding country. On our left as we advanced was timber; on our right a large plantation, a two-storey frame-house, painted white, standing back from the road some three hundred yards; between the house and main road the ground was covered with a dense growth of live-oaks and silver-poplars, completely hiding from the house the view of any passing column.

Two roads wended their way through this little forest from the main road to the house, one above and the other below it, taking an oblique direction. It appears that when the column was stopped, the advance was just opposite the house, and while waiting for further developments from the scouts, several men under command of Lieutenant Gaston, company G, Seventh Illinois, proceeded to the house. As they rode up to the gate they were surprised at seeing four armed rebels standing around in the yard, their horses being tied outside the gate. The "rebs" were surprised as well, and both parties showed a disposition to fight. Our men demanded their surrender, which they had no notion of complying with.

Both parties commenced firing upon each other, which resulted in our men taking two, putting the other two to flight, and an easy capture of the four horses. One of our men was struck in the breast by a buck-shot, striking one of his ribs and glancing off without inflicting a serious wound. This explained the firing while at the picket-post, and these four "rebs "belonged to that post, but had gone to the house to procure something to eat, not expecting the "Yanks "to come that way. They paid little or no attention to their duty.

I was again ordered to proceed cautiously, and upon reaching the place where we had taken in the picket I thought I could see two mounted men off to my right, in an oblique direction, and about one quarter of a mile off; an open field was between us, having a gradual descent towards them. On surveying the road with my eye I could see that after following it for a quarter of a mile it turned a right angle, and then at the distance of another quarter it entered the timber, at which point those two men appeared sitting on their horses, and not moving but looking very earnestly at us. That a force was down in the bottom, and that not very far off, was pretty well understood; but what that force was, and their number, we did not know, but, as the game says, we had to "go it blind."

Leaving a man at this point with instructions to stop the column, which could advance this far without being seen by those who appeared to be watching us from below, and at the same time see all that was going on in the bottom, outside of the timber, I proceeded with Stedman. Fowler and Wood had taken the right-hand road, and advanced on it about one hundred yards, when one of the horsemen cried out in a loud voice, "What in h—l does all that firing mean?"

I answered that reinforcements were coming up, and that his picket had fired on our advance, thinking that they were "Yanks," but no one was hurt, and it was all right.

At this one of them broke out in a roar of laughter, and said "Is that all?" and putting spurs to his horse started towards us at a gallop, leaving his comrade behind. I told Fowler to let him ride up between us, and I would manage him. Each one of us carried our revolvers in our hands ready for instant use. Up he came, looking much pleased, and said, "How are you, boys; how much force have you got?"

We had now halted, and as he rode in between us I turned my horse in an oblique direction, changing my revolver into my left hand, cocked it, and pointing it at his breast, attracted his attention to it, and in a quiet way told him not to speak or make a motion, but hand over his arms to Fowler or I would blow him through; he at once complied, though not without some astonishment at our proceedings. I then directed my attention to "reb" number two, and discovered that he was coming slowly towards us. Stedman, who had dismounted for some reason, was leading his horse and advancing to meet him. He had returned his revolver to its holster, feeling confident that he had an easy prey. They met about one hundred yards from where I was then standing. Stedman was so anxious to secure his man that he forgot for a moment the character he was to play, which came near proving fatal to him. As they met Stedman let go his bridle-rein and grasped that of his opponent, at the same time laying his hand firmly on his revolver holster and ordered him to surrender.

This proceeding somewhat confused the "reb's" ideas, and for a moment he did not know what to think, at the same time he looked up the hill and must have seen the column advancing. He was a large, athletic man, while Stedman was very small. With a quick movement he tried to release the hold Stedman had on his holster, at the same time saying. "Who and what in h—l are you?" It only took a moment to see something was wrong, and calling to Wood to come on I put spurs to my horse, and in a few moments was presenting a revolver at his head, threatening to blow his brains out if he did not surrender; he at once complied. I could not but admire his manly proportions, and face beaming with courage and bravery. I noticed the gold bars on his collar, which in the Southern army denotes captain. I ordered him to follow me, and told him not to be alarmed, that we were Illinois boys and he would be treated well.

Smilingly he said, in a clear, firm voice, "I am not afraid, sir; I would not have been your prisoner had it not been that I was deceived in your dress." He proved to be a Captain Scott, and commanded the force then within rifle-shot.

Just at this time Colonel Blackburn came galloping up, alone, and said to me, "Sergeant, bring along your scouts and follow me, and I'll see where those rebels are." I called one of my men and told him to take the captain back to the column, which by this time had descended the hill, and were advancing within four hundred yards of us. I then started, followed by Kelly, Wilson and Wood. The colonel being some distance ahead we had to increase our speed to a gallop to overtake him. It seemed to me that this was a rash movement on the part of Colonel Blackburn, but he had ordered me to follow him, and it was my duty to obey. As soon as we reached the spot where the two horsemen were first seen, we were at the end of a lane, and a few yards further all was timber. A considerable stream of water could be seen wending its way through the marshy and heavily timbered bottom. A little to the left, about seventy-five yards, is the crossing, a narrow plank bridge, some fifty feet in length, better known as Wall's Bridge, across the Trickafaw River, in Hunt County, and within one mile of Wall's post-office.

Just before we reached the bridge we were saluted by a few shots fired from the opposite side of the stream, which did not check our speed, but rather increased it. Closely following Colonel Blackburn all dashed upon the bridge, but ere the last one of us had reached the opposite side we were greeted by a loud volley of carbines and musketry, coming from some eighty of Colonel Wirt Adams' cavalry, who lay in ambush not more than fifty yards distant. It seemed as though a flame of fire burst forth from every tree. The colonel fell, along with his horse, both pierced by the fatal bullet. One of my comrades had his horse shot under him. A minnie ball struck me on my right thigh, passing through it into my saddle, just grazing my horse's back. Three shots were all I could get. I began to feel a faintness creeping over me, but still clinging to my revolver I turned my horse about and tried to retrace my steps amid the flying bullets.

When the first few shots were fired it was heard by Colonel Grierson, who then occupied the advance, and was the advance guard of the column. On they came, most gallantly, led by Lieutenant Styles, who charged across the bridge, followed by only twelve men. No sooner over the bridge than they were checked by a well directed volley. They rally and charge, but it is useless—they were too few and exposed, while the enemy were protected by the surrounding timber. The little band have to retreat back across the bridge, leaving one man killed and two wounded, and seven dead horses. They had no support; the column was too far behind to lend assistance in time, but just as they re-crossed the bridge the column came up on the double-quick.

Colonel Prince, by order of Colonel Grierson, ordered companies A and D of his regiment to dismount. They were sent to the right and left as skirmishers. One section of Captain Smith's battery was brought up, the woods were shelled, the enemy put to flight, and our men were pursuing them, and as they pass Colonel Blackburn, who laid mortally wounded, with one leg under his horse, cries out to them, "Onward! follow them, boys!" and cheers. The Sixth now take the advance—no halt is made—the Seventh look after the killed and wounded; they are all borne by friendly hands, and with tender care placed in the ambulances and carried forward one mile and left at the plantation of Mr. Newman. Their horses, equipments and arms are turned over to comrades and friends to take through with them. Many a kind farewell was given, and friends parted, some never to meet again on this side of the grave.

The following are the casualties sustained at this place, all belonging to the Seventh Illinois: Lieut.-Col. Blackburn, mortally wounded; Quartermaster-Sergeant of the regiment, R. W. Surby, flesh-wound; William Roy, Company G, seriously; R. W. Hughes, Company G, mortally; and Geo. Reinhold, Company G, killed. The following members were left to nurse and attend to the wants of the wounded: Serg't-Maj. A. Le Suer, Seventh Illinois; George W. Douglass, Company A, Seventh Illinois; and Dr. Yole—whose services were very valuable—of the Second Iowa Cavalry, who accompanied the expedition.

And now, as my thoughts at that time were with the command, thinking of their safety, with the reader's permission, I will still continue to be with them, until they again return to old Tennessee, and then, not forgetful of the sufferings of those who we were compelled to leave behind, will return and tell you of their fate.

The Sixth was pursuing the fast retreating foe, for they began to scatter in all directions. It was amusing to see some of them grasping their horses' manes, while their lower extremities were half suspended in the air; their saddle-girths have broken, and off tumbles saddle and blanket, leaving the rider bare-backed, with his legs pressed close to his horse's sides, his body thrown forward, resting upon his neck, and bare-headed. Occasionally a ball whizzes past him; he is fortunate enough if he escapes capture. The road is strewn with old saddles, blankets, coats, hats, and firearms. It was rarely we participated in such a chase; but it is not quite so fine when the joke is on the other side.

While we are enjoying the prospect of such a chase I will go back to the scene of the last few hours and endeavour to show you how, in my opinion, the loss of our few brave hearts could have been avoided.

You will remember of reading, a few pages back, of the manner in which I approached the picket-post, accompanied by two of my men, and how, just as I was on the eve of obtaining information respecting the forces in the bottom, and whose command, that a few shots were heard at the house on our right; it was those shots that frustrated our plans and left us in the dark. Had Lieutenant Gaston and squad not entered the house, thereby meeting the enemy, firing upon each other and giving the alarm, all would have no doubt ended well. With the information I should have obtained from the picket it would have been sufficient for Colonel Grierson to so perfected his plans as to have surprised the enemy and taken them prisoners, and that very probably without the loss of life, thereby still securing to the country a few good soldiers, a brave and efficient field-officer, and prevented the sorrow and anguish that was inflicted on the loved ones at home.

Another sad mistake was that Lieut.-Colonel Blackburn, unfortunately with too much daring, proceeded across the bridge with no other support than a few scouts. He being a very large man, dressed in full uniform, and mounted upon a very fine horse, was a most conspicuous mark. There was no call for this movement. The scouts had performed their duty up to this time, and having every assurance that the enemy was nearby they should have been withdrawn, at least long enough to have changed their costume; however, it is all past, and I often think that it was a miracle that any of us escaped the first volley; but the ways of Divine Providence are very mysterious, and I have every reason to be thankful that my fate was no worse.

We will now see how the advance is progressing. The command was now in Louisiana, Amit County being the last county passed through in Mississippi. We found the roads in good condition, and were making not less than six miles per hour. It was about two o'clock, p.m., the column was about six miles from Wall's Bridge, and the scouts, who were in the advance, discovered off to the right about forty rebels advancing on a side road leading into the main one. The scouts made a halt at this corner and fired several shots, which was replied to by the "rebs," who still kept advancing, seeming determined to gain the main road, but ere they could accomplish this the Sixth came in sight, and at the distance of six hundred yards brought one of their guns into position and threw a few shells among them, which had the desired effect, causing them to beat a hasty retreat.

This was most opportune, for had they gained the main road nothing could have prevented them from reaching the Amit River and effectually destroying the extensive bridge over that stream, which would have resulted most seriously with us. About four p.m. the command passed through Greensborough, a small town in St. Helena County. It was here that Lieutenant Newall, company G, Sixth Illinois, overtook the command, having been sent early that morning with a few men to procure horses and provisions. He was not aware of the fight until he had passed over the battle-ground, which somewhat increased his speed until he overtook the column. He had a narrow escape from being captured.

As the scouts entered this place Samuel Nelson discovered a mounted "reb," who was armed with a shot-gun, and apparently standing picket on a cross-road. Samuel approached him, and saluting him inquired who he was and what he was doing there. He replied that he was the County Clerk, and was waiting for a courier to come up that he might learn the news. Samuel then asked him if he knew who he was talking too. The fellow replied that he did not remember of seeing him before, but thought he was a soldier and belonged to Port Hudson. Samuel says, "No, sir; you are mistaken—you are talking to a live Yankee, and here is some Yankee whisky." "Reb" looked somewhat surprised at first, but displayed good taste and judgment— took the proffered canteen, and raising it to his lips took a good drink. As soon as the column came up Samuel turned him over, but before they parted company he very politely asked Samuel for "another nip of that Yankee whisky." Of course Samuel gave it to him, and he appeared to be very well satisfied with his new quarters.

On leaving town the column took a southwest course, and met with nothing of note until they had gone about four miles, when the scouts brought in two couriers, who were on their way to Osyko Station. The column was now proceeding on a good road, level as a floor, beautifully shaded on both sides by tall forest pines, interspersed with a small growth of other kinds of timber, now and then passing a small plantation, until within four miles of Amit River, when the country became more open, displaying considerable cultivation and some fine residences, with extensive plantations.

The night was a clear, starlight one, and moderately warm, the moon not making its appearance until about eleven o'clock, which added to the beauty of the surrounding country. Yet there was little interest displayed in the scenery, the men being too much exhausted for want of rest, and nearly every man was nodding as he rode along, reminding me of the old song, "Nid, nid, nodding." For the last hour previous to reaching the Amit River considerable delay was occasioned by waiting for the scouts, who were ordered to visit different plantations and obtain all the information they could respecting the situation of the bridge and whether any force was stationed there.

Before reaching the bridge the scouts learned that a post of couriers was stationed during the day, and at night withdrawn, one half mile from the bridge, on the south side of the river. If this should prove to be the case, what a considerable advantage would be gained? Once across this bridge and all was comparatively safe. So thought Colonel Grierson, who was fully awake to the interests of his command. When within one mile of the bridge the roads became very muddy and rough.

The column was halted, and the scouts were ordered to proceed to the bridge and ascertain if any picket was stationed there. Samuel taking the advance arrived at the bridge, dismounted and proceeded across on foot. The bridge was about two hundred yards in length, over a deep and rapid stream. He found it all right, and was not long in reporting this good news to Colonel Grierson, who gave the order "Forward!" and in a few minutes the horse's hoofs could be heard rattling upon the planks.

It was a striking scene to witness the column crossing this long bridge at the hour of midnight. After crossing the column passed through a delightful country. The distance from the Amit to the Comit River is seventeen miles, and better roads are seldom travelled in the interior of any state. No alarm had been given in crossing the bridge. The couriers, who numbered ten men, were asleep at a house about half a mile from the bridge, little dreaming that the Yankee raiders were then within rifle-shot.

They were not disturbed, and not until daylight did they learn what a rich prize had escaped their vigilance. For the first few hours every man was aroused, and all were congratulating each other on the success of the expedition. All felt that they were comparatively safe, and occasionally could be heard the booming of the mortars, which were throwing their ponderous shells into Port Hudson, all of which had a tendency to inspire the men with the prospect of soon meeting with our forces; thus we continued to move along, meeting with no obstacle.

On crossing the bridge over Big Sandy Creek the scouts discovered a camp not more than two hundred yards from the bridge, but could not discover any sentinels, and upon approaching nearer saw two negroes, who were busy building a fire. Without being seen the scouts withdrew and reported to Colonel Grierson, who immediately ordered Lieut.-Col. Loomis to send forward two companies of the Sixth to open fire, while the rest of the regiment brought up the rear. Captain Marshall, company H, dismounted his men, crossed the bridge silently—being supported by Captain Lynch, with company E, mounted—and when within one hundred yards raised a tremendous yell, shooting and charging down through the long rows of tents, which must have somewhat startled the unconscious sleepers, who felt so perfectly secure as not to have out any pickets. Instead of finding a considerable force here, as was expected, there were only about forty men, principally convalescents, nearly all of whom were captured.

The force stationed at this place numbered six hundred, (Williams' cavalry.) They had the day previous to this been ordered to push forward to Brookhaven and intercept the Yankees. Colonel Grierson at once ordered Colonel Prince to move forward on the advance, while the Sixth stopped long enough to destroy the camp and garrison equipage, and secure the prisoners, one of whom escaped and was afterwards captured, and related his experience that night by stating that he rushed from his tent, reached his horse, sprang upon his back, and away he went, bare-backed, with nothing on but his shirt and drawers and socks; he never stopped until he reached home, some sixty miles distant. The only casualty that happened while capturing this place was the wounding of one rebel.

We will now follow the Seventh, who are in the advance, going at a lively pace, over a good road, which began to show some signs of dust. The morning was beautiful, with a clear sky and a bright sun. The country had the appearance of being very level—on our right somewhat low and swampy, for several miles on our left fine and extensive plantations. After proceeding about a mile and a half a single horseman was seen, by two member's of company A, to emerge into the road about two hundred yards in their advance, and between them and the scouts. The road was so straight and level that most any moving object could be seen for the distance of two miles. As soon as he came into the road he was ordered to halt, but did not feel inclined to obey orders, and using his spurs away he dashed, hotly pursued, exchanging a few shots. In a few minutes he overtakes our scouts, whom he takes for some of his own men, and brandishing his revolver over and around his head excitedly says, "Get out of here, boys; the road is full of 'Yanks' in our rear!"

"Yes," says one of the scouts, as they closed in around him, "and you are right among them now." Imagine his surprise.

His name was Hinson, and a lieut.-col. of cavalry. He had heard the firing in the direction of the camp that morning, and was on his way to give notice to a picket-post between them and Baton Rouge. After proceeding about three miles Samuel Nelson, who was somewhat in advance of his companions, met a man walking, a citizen, and asked him if there were any soldiers around. He replied that there was one at the next house, about a quarter of a mile further, on the right-hand side of the road.

Samuel pushed ahead and stopped in front of the house. Dismounting and stepping up to the door, which was wide open, he confronted a female, who very politely invited him to enter. On stepping into the room he saw a soldier and three females seated around a table, enjoying a meal. The lady invited him to partake of their hospitality, which invitation he very readily accepted, and while eating had a very lively conversation with the "reb," from whom he learned that there was a company stationed on the road about four miles from there. After Samuel had got all the information he wanted from the "reb," he asked him where he belonged. He answered that he was a lieutenant, and his command was at Natchez. Samuel then said, "You may consider yourself my prisoner."

The lieutenant, feeling very indignant, replied, "I am an officer, sir, and will start for my command in the morning; besides, sir, you have nothing to do with me, if you are a conscripting officer."

At this one of the women spoke and said, "He ain't no officer and can't conscript you."

Samuel, turning to the officer, said, "Do you know who you are talking to?"

"I suppose you are a soldier, sir," replied the lieutenant.

"Yes, sir," said Samuel, "and a live Yankee, and you may just consider yourself my prisoner."

At this the ladies burst forth in a chorus of voices, "It ain't no such thing; you can't fool us; don't believe him; he ain't nothing but a common soldier."

Just at this time a squad of company A appeared in front of the house, to which he pointed. This changed the aspect of affairs; they all at once comprehended the meaning of the blue coats, and with tears and screams they all commenced hugging the lieutenant, exclaiming, "Oh, my dear, they will kill you, they will kill you."

Samuel quieted their fears by telling them that not a hair of his head should be harmed, and giving the lieutenant in charge of the orderly-sergeant of company A, again took his place in the advance, though not before reporting to Colonel Grierson the information he had obtained respecting the force ahead. Nothing occurred until the column had arrived within half a mile of the Comit River, at which place the force spoken of was expected to be found. The scouts were ordered to advance cautiously and reconnoitre the ground, and find out the position of the camp. Owing to the situation of the ground the scouts could approach to within three hundred yards of the camp without being seen, the enemy not having out any vidette on that side, and as yet no report had reached them of the Yankees coming that way. The scouts then halted, and Wood volunteered to go and reconnoitre and see what he could discover.

Just then a soldier was seen coming up from the creek, and approaching the scouts said, "How are you, gentlemen; have you come to relieve us?"

"Yes; the company will be up in a few minutes."

"It's about time you come to relieve us; we've been here now four days, and are just about out of rations."

The scouts told him they would soon be relieved. In the meantime Wood returned, having obtained all desired information. The camp was situated along the east bank of the stream, shaded by timber, just at the end of the lane, and could not be approached only by charging down the road, which was fenced on either side. After the scouts had reported to Colonel Grierson the command moved forward slowly until within three hundred yards of the camp, when the following companies were ordered to proceed: company A to flank through the field on the left, while companies D, E and I kept the road, the former commanded by Lieutenant Bradshaw, the latter by Captain Ashmead. They charged most gallantly upon the unsuspecting foe.

So complete was the surprise that the rebels, forgetting everything, tried to seek safety in flight; but a very few of them escaped, and not more than a dozen shots were fired. The confusion was indescribable—shot-guns, saddles, camp-kettles, rifles, old blankets, coats and hats scattered in all directions, while men and loose horses were stampeding from all quarters. It did not take long for our men to flank the woods and pick up the stragglers. One man, a member of company I, found sixteen rebels hid in a hole that the water had washed out by the bank of the stream. They all surrendered to him. While the Seventh was thus engaged gathering up their booty the Sixth was ordered in the advance, so as to save time.

It was now about nine o'clock, a.m., and in half an hour's time the Seventh followed the Sixth, having captured forty-two prisoners belonging to Stewart's cavalry, together with all their horses and equipments, without sustaining any loss or damage. In order to cross this stream the command had to move up its bank about a half mile and ford it. All those owning large horses had the advantage—they could ford it without swimming, while the small ones had to resort to the latter extremity. After proceeding three miles the whole command stopped to rest and feed, the first for man or horse for the last thirty hours, having traveled eighty miles night and day, with scarcely a halt, and it is to be remembered that nearly the whole command was asleep on their horses while marching the greater portion of the last night.

The command was now within six miles of Baton Rouge, and all felt quite safe. The raid had been one grand success. A kind Providence had smiled upon our efforts all through our perilous journey, and finally crowned it with victory. Nearly eight hundred miles had been travelled in sixteen days, passing through fourteen counties, and through the interior of the State of Mississippi, destroying a great amount of government property, besides the destruction of railroad property, and effectually cutting off communication in various directions, preventing supplies from reaching Vicksburg and Port Hudson, drawing out a force from Jackson, at a time when General Grant was making a rapid flank movement on that place, and on the last morning surprising two camps, capturing and bringing in four hundred prisoners, not including the six hundred that were paroled and left on the route at different points, besides eight hundred horses and mules, and some five hundred negroes that followed us, a large number of cattle, and a considerable train of vehicles of various descriptions.

But what must be considered the crowning glory of the expedition is the fact that during the entire march, and more especially the last forty hours, men and horses hungry and jaded though they were, not a murmur was heard from the lips of either officers or men. Our loss did not exceed twenty men.

While feeding and resting a company of the First Louisiana Cavalry, Union forces, came out from Baton Rouge, the report having reached there that a large force was crossing Comit River and advancing towards that place. This company was sent out to reconnoitre. Picture their astonishment when they learned whose command it was, and where it came from. It was some time before they could be convinced of the fact.

Our prisoners felt quite jubilant. They allowed that a force had to come all the way from Tennesse purposely to capture them; they considered it an honour to be taken by Illinois troops. Altogether they were a jolly set of fellows—the most of them living in Louisiana and Mississippi, and men of wealth. Their captain, at the time their camp was taken, escaped by climbing a tree, where he remained concealed by the Spanish moss, which abounds in that section of the country, and presents a beautiful sight, hanging in long clusters from every limb.

About eleven o'clock the command took up its line of march in the following order: first, the Sixth Illinois; second, the battery; third, the prisoners; fourth, the Seventh Illinois; fifth, the negroes, with the led horses and mules; and lastly, about thirty vehicles of every description, from the finest carriage down to a lumber wagon of the poorest description. The line extended about two miles. It really presented an interesting sight, one to which neither pen nor pencil can do justice.

After being formed, and when within four miles of Baton Rouge, the column was met by Captain Godfry, First Louisiana Cavalry, who escorted us into the city. For one half mile before entering the city we were met by citizens and soldiers, both white and black; male and female, old and young, rich and poor, paper collars and ragged urchins; everybody's curiosity was at its highest pitch. The streets were densely crowded, and amid the shouts and cheers of thousands, the waving of banners and flags, interspersed with music, the tired soldiers, all covered with dust, marched through the principal streets, around the public square, down to the river, watered their horses, and then proceeded to Magnolia Grove, two miles south of the city, a most delightful spot, shaded by the magnolia, whose long green leaves encircle a beautiful white flower, which fills the air with its rich perfume.

It was just at sunset that the command entered this grove, and that night, for the first time in sixteen days, they slept soundly under federal protection. Among the sleepers were the scouts—except those left behind now—relieved of their dangerous double-dealing duty, which rendered their death certain if they had been taken prisoners and discovered. They had given full satisfaction to the command, and I trust will make a favourable impression upon the mind of the reader. Their names are as follows:

R. W. Surby, Regimental Q. M. Sergeant, Seventh Illinois, commanding scouts; C. B. Weeden, corporal Co. E, do; L. H. Kelly, Co. E, do; Wm. Buffington, Co. B, do; Samuel Nelson, Co. G, do; Arthur Wood, Co. B, do; Isaac E. Robinson, Co. B, do; George Stedman, Co. C, do; Uriah Fowler, Co. H, do.

They were armed in guerrilla style, with a variety of arms—three Sharpe's carbines, four shot-guns, one sporting rifle, four sabres, and nine revolvers; had captured eighty-four prisoners, with their arms and equipments, and destroyed over two hundred shot-guns and rifles.

The evening found the men so exhausted for want of sleep and rest that the moment they had stripped the saddles off their horses they laid down, and it was almost impossible to arouse them, to partake of coffee and refreshments, prepared by the One Hundred and Sixteenth New York and the Forty-Eighth Mississippi Infantry regiments, who made their appearance, bringing with them their own cooking-utensils and provisions. This act on the part of the officers and men of those regiments was noble and kind, and will always be remembered by the Sixth and Seventh Illinois Cavalry.

On our entrance into Baton Rouge it was difficult to distinguish the prisoners from our own men, who had, while on the march, exchanged their close-fitting jackets for citizens' coats—the same with regard to hats and pants; this, together with the dust that covered them, made it impossible to distinguish them apart, and as the column marched along the following remarks were heard: "Why, see how many prisoners they have!" A group of negroes was seen on one corner of the street, in which an old darkey was heard to say to one of his brethren, "Hush, child; you must look at dem peoples with respect; dey am de great warriors, wat come from de Norf; dey trable widout sleep, and stop de railroads, and cut up de track; I hear massa say so dis mornin'."

While on our route we were looked upon by the people with wonder and astonishment, and our courteous and kind manners seemed to surprise them considerably. There were undoubtedly instances where some unprincipled men would enter private dwellings, while away from the control of their officers, and pillage. Such things could not well be controlled, as the column was almost constantly on the move, and subsistence had to be procured from the country through which we passed. It was seldom we found a scarcity. Horses had to be pressed whenever and wherever found, and in many instances double the number were left for those taken, of exhausted animals, which, with a little care, would soon become as serviceable as those taken. It would sometimes arouse a feeling of regret to witness the attachment displayed by the faithful old horse, who, on being turned loose by the roadside, to wander where he pleased, would be seen following up the column, and when it stopped he would lay down in the road to rest, and as we started again could be seen occupying a place in the ranks, where he would remain from morning to night, faithful in the discharge of his duty.

After a few days' rest the command began to wander around. They being privileged characters, were permitted to go where they pleased, and it was amusing to see to what extent they would carry their jokes. At one time they took possession of the provost marshal's office, turning him out of doors. One day about a dozen men went into a saloon—the proprietor having stepped out for a moment. Without waiting for him one of the men jumped over the counter and inquired of his comrades what they would have, and thus they treated each other until the proprietor arrived. He was refused admittance. For redress he applied to the provost marshal, who recommended him to shut up shop, that he could not do anything with those raiders.

At another time some of the men entered an ice-cream saloon, and were rather noisy, when the provost marshal was sent for. The men got "wind" of it, and taking the soda fount charged it with gas and placed it in position opposite the door. The marshal made his appearance, and would have received a salute had not a friend outside advised him of the danger. He very readily compromised with the men. Occasionally they would get into a fight, just for the fun of the thing. Passing an eating-house one day three of the men were attracted by hearing loud and angry words. Their curiosity must be satisfied. They entered the house and discovered two eastern officers engaged in a fist-fight. The landlady was trying her utmost to prevent the quarrel, and as our men entered entreated them to stop it if they could, as such a proceeding would injure the reputation of her house, which was of unquestionable character. Western troops are noted for their gallantry, and in less than no time the two officers lay sprawling in the street.

It is customary in Baton Rouge, when an auction is to take place, also for concerts and other entertainments, to send a negro around with a banner with the advertisement, and a bell, which he rings, and cries out at the top of his voice. As one of these was coming up the street one day a squad of the Sixth and Seventh made a charge, capturing the bell and banner. They proceeded on through the streets, crying out "Concert tonight, at Magnolia Grove, by the Sixth and Seventh Illinois Cavalry." Some of the citizens were sold that evening. Providing they ever do conclude to give a concert, I have composed the following few lines for their benefit:

SONG OF THE RAIDERS.

The Sixth and Seventh you all know,
Du da, du da,
Together on the raid did go;
Row de du da da,
Colonel Grierson was in command,
Du da, du da,
And in Baton Rouge did safely land,
Row de du da da.

Chorus—

Are you going to march all night?
Are you going to march all day?
I'll bet my money on the Sixth and Seventh,
Who'll bet on the Southern Grey?

It was in April, 1863,
Du da, du da,
That we left the State of Tennessee;
Row de du da da;
The course we took on the map you'll see,
Du da, du da,
Down through the State of Mississippi,
Row de du da da.

Chorus.

We were accompanied part way,
Du da, du da,
By the brave old Second Iowa;
Row de du da da;
When at Clear Spring they were left to range,
Du da, du da,
And fight their way back to La Grange,
Row de du da da.

Chorus.

With the railroad we did play "whack,"
Du da, du da,
Burning the cars upon the track;
Bow de du da da;
We'd march all day and then all night,
Du da, du da,
And only stop to have a fight,
Row de du da da.

Chorus.

The people thought it very strange,
Du da, du da,
To see so many from La Grange;
Row de du da da;
They looked with wonder and surprise,
Du da, du da,
To see so many from Illinois,
Row de du da da.

Chorus.

When Port Hudson did surrender,
Du da, du da,
We were there to see the "rebs" knock under;
Row de du da da;
The 116th New York are bully boys,
Du da, du da,
Kind hearted and full of fight besides,
Row de du da da.

Chorus.

And now, kind friends, we'll bid adieu,
Du da, du da,
Hoping to see this war soon through;
Row de du da da;
How joyful then will be our song,
Du da, du da,
As our wings of peace will glide along,
Row de du da da.

Chorus—

    Are you going to march all night?

Are you going to march all day?
I'll bet my money on the Stars and Stripes,
On Freedom and Liberty.

The following is characteristic of the good feeling existing between the Sixth and Seventh. One day one of the men, in roving around, discovered two men fighting. Stepping up to them he said, "How is this, Sixth and Seventh? you must not fight each other in this style."

At this announcement the combatants eyed each other a moment, when one says to the other, "Do you belong to the Seventh?"

"I do; and you to the Sixth, do you?"

"Well, I reckon I do," was the reply. This was sufficient, and like two brothers they started, arm in arm, to the nearest saloon, to pledge anew their friendship for each other, allowing it was all a mistake.

About this time several of the officers, with Colonel Grierson and Prince, went on a visit to New Orleans. On their arrival in that city they were received by the citizens, who displayed considerable interest, complimenting them for their bravery and success, and as a token of their admiration for their gallantry, the one was presented with a horse and equipments, the other with equipments.

This state of things was not permitted to last long. The Illinois cavalry had their reputation up for being fighting men, and work was now laid out for them. The bombardment of Port Hudson had commenced, and a movement was to be made against the place by a land force. On the twelfth day of May the cavalry was ordered to move in the advance to Port Hudson. Some considerable skirmishing took place with the advance, until within eight miles of Port Hudson, at which point our forces, under General Auger, camped, and remained some time before advancing again.

During this time the cavalry was not idle. A scout was made, which reflected great credit both upon the officers and men concerned. Captain Godfry, of the First Louisiana Cavalry, with one company, Captain Angley, of the Sixth Illinois, with one company, and Lieutenant La Grange, of company A, with twenty men, were sent from Alexandria eight miles to the rear of Port Hudson. When in the vicinity of the latter place, they learned of there being a force of rebels there, numbering ninety men. The three commands then separated, each taking a different road, with the intention of surrounding them.

Captain Angley had succeeded in drawing the rebels after him, and falling back to a suitable position held them in check, while Lieutenant La Grange, learning of their situation, charged down upon them in the rear, completely surprising them, killing two and capturing nineteen prisoners, with their arms, horses and equipments, without sustaining any loss.

A few days after this the entire force was ordered to advance, which brought on the engagement at Plain's Store, noted for its stubbornness. Major Whitsit, of the Sixth Illinois, with companies A, K and L, were sent up to the railroad from the store, meeting the enemy—Colonel Miles' Legion—and commenced the engagement, falling back to the reserve, the enemy following closely. When the battle became general the Forty-eighth Massachusetts and One Hundred and Sixteenth New York behaved most gallantly, the latter regiment doing most of the fighting, the cavalry affording good support, dismounted. The fight lasted seven hours, when the enemy was driven from his position, leaving their killed and wounded on the field, which numbered one hundred, besides sixty prisoners. Our loss was fifty-four killed and wounded.

The next day General T. W. Sherman, of the east, arrived from New Orleans, with a long train of heavy artillery. On the following morning the Sixth and Seventh were ordered out, at an early hour. After riding about an hour they met the advance of General Banks' force, which had come up the west side of the river from New Orleans, and crossed to Bayou Sara. The first meeting which then took place between General Banks and Colonel Grierson was very warm and friendly. On the twenty-first of May a demonstration was made by our forces against the enemy, who were in position outside their works. It was here the One Hundred and Sixteenth New York distinguished themselves, repulsing the enemy, charging and driving them inside their works, while a Massachusetts regiment threw down their arms and run. The cavalry being ordered to dismount and support the New York regiment caused much surprise in the stampeders; they had never heard of such a thing as cavalry fighting dismounted.

On the twenty-fourth of May our forces advanced to within one mile of the fort. Some heavy skirmishing was done in the advance. Several attempts had been made by our forces to discover two steamers said to be concealed up the bayou, or Thompson's Creek, but were unsuccessful. Colonel Prince, by order of Colonel Grierson, left with detachments from each company of his regiment, proceeding to the creek, where he captured two fine passenger steamers, the *Skylight*, also a small ferry-boat. These boats lay within three hundred yards of the rebel batteries. So quiet and unexpected was the expedition that they were completely surprised, and knew nothing of it until the boats were run up the creek out of range of the guns. Colonel Prince was highly complimented by General Banks, who pronounced it one of the grandest feats of the campaign.

The next day Lieutenant Lee, of company F, with four men, took a yawl belonging to one of the steamers and quietly dropped down the creek, passed close to the rebel works, entered Alligator Bayou, which they crossed, landed, and footing it through a neck of timber hailed the steamship *Hartford*. A yawl was lowered and they were brought aboard, and reported the capture of the boats, which the Hartford had been watching for at the outlet, to prevent their escape. Lieutenant Lee was highly complimented and kindly treated by the officers of the boat, and three cheers were given for the Illinois cavalry.

The men had considerable sport while camped in the rear of Port Hudson shooting alligators, with now and then a skirmish with Logan's or Wirt Adams' cavalry. In the meantime our forces were encircling and drawing nearer the enemy's works, the cannonading was growing more fierce and terrific each day, and sharp-shooting was practiced to some extent. Many of our cavalry could be seen each day on their way to the rifle-pits near the Twenty-first Indiana Battery, where they would dispose of fifty or a hundred cartridges before returning, firing at the distance of six hundred yards.

It was on the last day of May that the enemy charged one of our siege-guns, but we easily repulsed them. By the middle of June our forces had nearly two hundred guns in position, and the cannonading was most terrific. The heavy siege battery manned by the Twenty-first Indiana, Colonel McMiller, proved most efficient. So accurate became their aim that the rebels dared not place a gun within their range. On the fourteenth of June our forces, commanded by General Sherman, made a desperate charge upon the enemy's works, and were repulsed with some loss. Captain Skinner, of the Sixth Illinois, with companies E and D of that regiment, was escort for the general. Their loss in horses was seventeen. The general had two shot from under him, and was himself carried off the field wounded. A braver or more gallant officer never led troops into any engagement.

It was on one of these occasions that a certain Massachusetts regiment refused to enter action because their time would be out in a few days. They were nine months' men. Previous to starting for their homes there was a great demand for trophies, and our cavalry could sell them almost anything for a good price. Many of the men took advantage and sold out, even to their old jack-knives, stating that they were captured on the raid.

The weather was now becoming excessively hot, and it was a severe task to both horses and men to labour through the heat of the day. In many instances scouts had to be postponed and conducted through the night. The large green flies and mosquitoes were very troublesome. The country abounded in blackberries, which afforded the men a luxury. Sugar could be obtained in abundance at the different plantations. Frequently the men approached the gun-boats, when some hearty old tar would hail them and inquire if they did not want to come aboard. They had a very exalted opinion of the cavalry, and looked upon them as true heroes. Regardless of the excessive heat, change of climate, and constant scouting, our men experienced but little sickness, and would find some kind of amusement to while away the spare hours.

Musical instruments of various kinds could be found in camp, and the most noted among the players was Colonel Grierson, who could produce most perfect music on nearly all instruments. He possesses a natural talent for music. On several occasions after retiring has he arisen from his bed on hearing a violin, and finding it out would have all the negroes collected, and then such a variety of dances the reader can better imagine than I describe—jigs, breakdowns, and the original plantation dance, with its chorus of voices. There could be seen Sambo in all his glory—the genuine African.

There are several fine plantations and beautiful residences in the rear of Port Hudson and above it, particularly that of Mrs. ——, a sister of Jeff. Davis. While on a scout Colonel Grierson had occasion to call and pay his respects to this lady, who received him rather coldly. Not knowing who the colonel was she very uncourteously left him and his adjutant alone in the drawing-room. In the room was a splendid piano. A request was made through the adjutant for the ladies to play, which they declined. The colonel was not to be bluffed in this way, so seating himself before the instrument he soon filled the room with the notes of a very difficult but popular air.

This had the desired effect of bringing all the ladies to the room. They were very inquisitive to know who the player was, that he would not be any ordinary man to produce such beautiful music. Upon hearing his name they evinced much surprise, and apologised for their rudeness, they became extremely sociable, particularly with Adjutant Woodward, who is a great favourite with the ladies; of very prepossessing appearance, (good looking,) and knows how to play the agreeable; he is unassuming and gentlemanly in his manners, and not fond of display, as the following will show. He was the only officer on Colonel Grierson's staff, acting adjt.-gen., and was of incalculable service. His judgment was consulted on all occasions. After the successful termination of the raid, he wrote the official report, in which he was so delicate as not to mention his own name.

A scout was sent out to Clinton, La., consisting of the following troops—the Sixth and Seventh, the Fourth Wisconsin Mounted Infantry, accompanied by Captain Godfry, Captain Eaton of the First Louisiana Cavalry, and Lieutenant Perkins of the Mississippi Cavalry. This expedition left within four miles of Port Hudson, marched twenty-eight miles, met the enemy in force, fought three hours and retreated in good order, on account of ammunition being exhausted, arriving in camp about three o'clock the next day. The day following an expedition consisting of cavalry, infantry and artillery returned to Clinton, but the enemy had disappeared, leaving in our possession one hundred convalescent soldiers, which were paroled by Colonel Prince. An extensive cotton factory was destroyed.

An attempt was made by the "rebs" to capture a boat, used for keeping supplies on at Springfield Landing. Captain Cohn, of the Sixth, and Lieutenant Maxwell, of the Seventh, were on board at the time, and rallied what few men, that were scattered about, which did not exceed twenty, and repulsed the "rebs," who numbered sixty men, driving them away.

Company E, of the Sixth, while on picket at the crossing of the Jackson and Clinton road, four and a half miles in rear of Port Hudson, was attacked by a superior force of the enemy. Sergeant Fayer was in command of the company at the time, and so placed his men as to hold the enemy in check while he sent a courier to camp, who returned with reinforcements, and the enemy were driven off. One battalion of the Fourteenth New York Cavalry, at this time, was stationed as picket on the cross-road and railroad. They had just received some clothing and three boxes of Colt's army revolvers. One hundred of the enemy attacked them, capturing several prisoners, nearly all their horses, their arms, clothing, and four wagons.

About a mile from this post was a hospital, in which were at this time about three hundred sick and wounded, with two companies of infantry acting as guard, six ambulances, a quantity of hospital stores, and one hundred stand of arms, all in charge of Surgeon ——, who surrendered the whole to a Confederate officer and four men. In the meantime news had reached camp. Lieutenants Maxwell and Caldwell, of the Seventh, immediately collected about twenty men, principally convalescents—the regiment being absent on a scout at the time—and started for the picket-post, where they arrived only to find the enemy gone with their booty.

They then started for the hospital, arriving in time to prevent its capture by the enemy, who had sent for reinforcements. The surgeon was very indignant, and insisted that he had surrendered the place, and would not permit the forces at his command to interfere. He soon found he had those to deal with who knew how to act, and with revolvers in hand Lieutenants Caldwell and Maxwell threatened to shoot the first man who refused to raise a musket in defence of his own liberty and Uncle Sam's property. Colonel Grierson, with his command, soon after made his appearance, who reprimanded the surgeon for his cowardly actions, but he was too late to pursue the enemy, they having sometime the start; they made good their escape, with the property taken from the Fourteenth New York Cavalry.

I will now draw the attention of the reader to those who were left wounded at Wall's Bridge, Mississippi. They had not been forgotten. Several efforts had been made by Colonel Prince to send a party with a flag of truce to learn their condition. *Madame* rumour was busy with her tongue. At one time she reported that Colonel Blackburn was dead, and that Sergeant Surby had been recognized as one of the scouts and was hung. It was about the last of June that permission was granted to proceed with a flag of truce, the rebel General Gardner furnishing the party with the necessary papers of protection. J. B. Hartley, company A, and A. G. Leving, veterinary-surgeon of the Seventh Illinois, started on their mission. They were to proceed to Clinton, Louisiana, where they were furnished with an escort of two Confederate soldiers, who accompanied them through.

On the afternoon of the second day they reached Mr. Newman's plantation, and found Mr. N. at home, but were disappointed in not finding any of the wounded. They were told that the colonel died, after suffering intense pain for seventeen days. A member of company G had also died from his wounds. The remaining two wounded men, together with the nurses, had been sent to Osyko Station. Mr. Newman expressed himself highly pleased and satisfied, stating that he had

FEDERAL CAVALRY ON A FORAGING EXPEDITION

been paid most liberally by all parties concerned, and also that the dead had received a decent burial, all of which was gratifying news to the friends of the deceased. On the morning of the fourth day the flag of truce returned, having made the trip without meeting with any accident or trouble on the road.

At one time Colonel Prince made an effort to he detached with his regiment from the Sixth Illinois without consulting Colonel Grierson, his intention being that of remaining in the Department of the Gulf. General Banks thought well of him, and appreciated his military genius, but the idea did not meet the approbation of the officers, all of whom opposed it with the exception of one, besides Colonel Grierson did not approve of it, and told the officers and men that he would take them back to Tennessee. Colonel Prince, in making this effort, thought it was to his interest. As a military man he has few superiors, and is perfectly conversant with the tactics.

The following is one of his ideas, suggested to General Banks, and by him and his chief engineer approved and carried into execution— that of collecting the. sugar hogsheads from the neighbouring plantations and constructing a lunette fort and tower of observation. This work was commenced by digging a trench within three hundred yards and following up to within forty-five yards of the enemy's works, when the main work was commenced as follows; thickness at the base, fifteen feet; length, forty feet; height, twenty feet; with wings extending from each flank, serving as rifle-pits. From the top of this a fine view was obtained of the enemy's river works, and was about to have been mounted with four guns, when the fort surrendered, which would have commanded an enfilading fire on both the enemy's flanks, which could not have been returned in the same manner by them. This work was frequently commented on, and General Gardner's chief-engineer remarked, that had it been completed, it would have proved very destructive to them.

When the news of the surrender of Vicksburg reached the command at Port Hudson, the rejoicing was beyond describing. On the eighth day of July General Gardner surrendered Port Hudson and its garrison to General Banks. It was then that the cannon pealed forth in thunder tones, volley after volley from the gunboats and land batteries in honour of the great victory achieved. The last stronghold on the Mississippi River was wrested from the traitor's clutch, the "father of waters" once more carried its entire length, proudly floating the banner of liberty. The next day a portion of our force marched into the fort, and then in the presence of cavalry, infantry, artillery and marines, the "rebs" grounded arms; this was a proud moment for the Illinois boys. General Gardner requested to see Colonel Grierson, who came forward and was introduced to him. He complimented the Colonel very highly, saying, that he was both glad and sorry to see him, glad to see so brave and gallant an officer, but sorry to see the one who caused the surrender of Port Hudson, he having cut off his communications and supplies, thus starving him into a surrender.

A few days after this the Sixth and Seventh embarked for Memphis, Tenn., amid the cheers of friends and the deafening roar of artillery. Accompanying and under guard, were the Confederate officers of the garrison, General Beall and staff occupying the same boat with Colonel Grierson and Colonel Prince. On our arrival at Vicksburg the boats were detained several hours, during which time Colonel Grierson had an interview with General Grant, who received him with marked courtesy, displaying a high appreciation of his services.

On the arrival of the command at Memphis, they disembarked, rejoicing that they had returned safely back again to old Tennessee, shortly after which a reunion took place between the raiders and those who were so unfortunate as to be left behind. They consisted mostly of convalescents and men who were on detached service, and doing duty at the time the expedition left, together with those who returned as an escort from near Pontotac, Miss., all of which did not spare them from a nickname conferred upon them by the raiders— "Quinine Brigade;" the meeting was warm between old comrades, and a thousand and one questions were asked, and a large mail was distributed, letters which contained word from the loved ones at home. Mails had been a scarce article while in the Department of the Gulf.

The brigade was once more thrown together, and the meeting between the Second Iowa and the Sixth and Seventh Illinois was of the most friendly character. The respect that these three regiments entertained toward each other is only what brave and unprejudiced minds are capable of; the confidence reposed in each other is generally portrayed on the battle field. I do not think I vary from the truth when I say the Second Iowa is the best drilled regiment in that branch of the service; in the department of the Mississippi, their fighting qualities were unquestionable, and with such a intrepit commander as Colonel Hatch they are invincible in an engagement. He knows how to get into a fight and how to get out again. The part they performed on the raid was of the greatest importance.

You will remember that this regiment left us and we proceeded alone, I will now give you their account of their journey back to La Grange. About five o'clock, April 21st, the column moved at the junction of the roads leading to Columbus, West Point and Louisville. At this point Colonel Grierson and Hatch separated, warmly shaking hands and mutually wishing each other God speed in their hazardous duties. In compliance with orders from Colonel Grierson, Colonel Hatch was to proceed with his regiment (about five hundred men and a section of artillery belonging to company K, First Illinois Light Artillery,) and make a demonstration toward Columbus, Miss., striking West Point; destroy the railroad bridge over the Okatibbayhaugh River; thence moved rapidly southward to Macon, destroying the railroad and government stores, and thence to find his way north to La Grange by the most direct route.

After the departure of Colonel Grierson, Colonel Hatch sent a detachment of his regiment with orders to follow the former about four miles, then counter march back for the purpose of obliterating the tracks of Colonel Grierson, then moving south; at the same time the Colonel ordered the pieces of artillery he had to be wheeled from the timber into the road four different times, so that the marks would correspond with the four pieces of artillery in Grierson's command; this done, Colonel Hatch moved rapidly until reaching Palo Alto, where he halted to feed and rest an hour. It was now about twelve o'clock. The enemy had been concentrating their forces several days previous, anticipating a movement on Columbus; their scouts had counted the entire column under Colonel Grierson; knowing the exact number they accumulated what they thought a sufficient force to overpower and capture the whole command.

Colonel Hatch had not separated from Grierson more than three hours, when the rebels who had been following in the rear made their appearance at the junction of the roads, and after patrolling a few miles in the direction that Colonel Grierson had gone, concluded from the counter marching that the main column had returned and gone toward Columbus. Under this impression they started in hot pursuit, and just as Colonel Hatch's command had finished their noonday meal they were most furiously attacked by a force under General Dolsen, consisting of Smith's partisan regiment, Bartoe's regiment and Ingis' battalion; on they came, confident of an easy victory, but the brave Iowa boys were not the least daunted. Company E and G quickly formed, and as the "rebs" came within easy range, poured a deadly volley from their running five shooting rifles, which quickly checked their speed and sent some of them to their long home.

They now fell back out of range and formed in two columns, moving down on both flanks. In the meantime Colonel Hatch quickly formed in the edge of the timber, where his devoted little band could be completely concealed by trees. With a portion of his force dismounted behind a barricade and breastwork constructed out of fence rails and logs; while the little two pounder was placed in a position to command the front, a sufficient force was placed on either flanks to protect the rear. In order to make the charge the "rebs" had to cross an open field; on they came the second time, yelling like demons'. Colonel Hatch had cautioned his men not to fire until the command was given. When within easy range the order "fire" was passed along the line.

At the command up rose two hundred men armed with the revolving rifle. Volley after volley was poured into the rebel ranks in quick succession, playing a tune more loud than charming, while the well manned cannon nobly supported the base. The rebels (who had boasted at a house near which they made the attack that they would take our cannon in three minutes,) did not appreciate this song and broke back in all directions. Colonel Hatch immediately ordered a charge which completely stampeded the entire command, driving them back full three miles, capturing thirty prisoners, besides about twenty-five killed and wounded men left on the field, and wonderful to tell not a drop of federal blood was spilt. From that time until dark it was a constant skirmish, the enemy still believing that they were engaging Grierson's entire command.

Colonel Hatch now shaped his course northward, crossing the Hooka River, and drawing the enemy's force immediately in his rear. On nearing the Tippah River it was discovered that the enemy were strongly posted on the opposite side to protect the ford. The Colonel at once turned into a large swamp through which the river run, and after, proceeding a few miles pressed in an old negro to act as guide. It was now near midnight and very dark. The guide led the command by a blind path to a ford crossing the river, one which had not been used in years. A place was found where a large quantity of floating timber had collected and was lodged against some trees; over this the men constructed a foot bridge, stripping their saddles off and carrying them over to the opposite side. The bank on the side where they entered the stream was about six feet high; the horses were pushed off this bank, one at a time, and compelled by long poles, used as whips, to swim to the opposite shore, where men stood hip deep in water to assist the animals up the bank which was too steep for them to climb unassisted; in this way the entire command crossed the river without any loss.

The cannon was taken to pieces and drawn over the bed of the stream by means of ropes. After crossing the command moved several miles before daylight, leaving the enemy, who were guarding the ford far in the rear. On the twenty-second the command took but little rest. Detachments were sent in various directions to hunt up droves of horses and mules, which had been run into the low bottom lands to avoid capture by our forces. The men sent out for this purpose were very successful. At four o'clock the command reached Okolona, a place on the Mobile and Ohio railroad, charging into town, driving out the enemy's cavalry and state troops, burning the barracks for five thousand troops, destroying a large quantity of ammunition, quartermaster's stores and considerable Confederate cotton. The command moved five miles northwest from town and camped for the night.

The twenty-third was spent hunting horses and mules. The enemy was again discovered trying to overtake the column. Citizens were collecting from all parts of the country armed with shot guns, hunting rifles, &c., constantly firing on the flanks of our troops, but taking care to keep at a respectful distance. Detachments were sent in various directions, which had the desired effect to so completely puzzle the enemy that they could not arrive at our real intended movement. In order to check the main force following in the rear, the bridge over the Chiroppa Creek was destroyed. The command camped for the night near Tupelo.

On the morning of the twenty-fourth Colonel Hatch sent Major Coon with six companies off to the left, to pursue another route and form a junction again near La Grange; while he, (the Colonel) with the remainder of the regiment and the plunder, consisting of thirty-one prisoners and over two hundred horses and mules, led by seventy negroes, took the Birmingham road. The rebels, who were constantly watching their movements, thought this their time, and just as the head of the column reached the latter named place the rebels attacked their rear in force. The colonel quickly detached a sufficient force to guard the prisoners and train; this done he had just sixty-five riflemen whom he could dismount, and fourteen sabre-men whom he placed on the flanks, mounted, and the little cannon manned by Corporal T.

H. Walker, Sixth Illinois Cavalry, and four men from the same regiment; with this small force the enemy was repulsed three times.

The colonel retreating slowly, concealing his men at all favourable points, letting them approach to within short range, when he would pour a withering fire into their exposed ranks with his revolving rifles, aided by the two pounder which did excellent service. The enemy suffered terribly, while the loss on our side was very small. In this way the attack was kept up for about six miles, when the enemy evidently became tired, and with exceptions of a little annoyance from guerilla parties they were not troubled by the enemy from that point to La Grange, where they arrived safe with all the plunder on the morning of the twenty-sixth.

The loss sustained by the Second Iowa Cavalry on this important trip was but ten men killed, wounded and missing. They left La Grange with seventy rounds of ammunition per man; on their return they had but two rounds left to the man. They captured and destroyed over three hundred shot-guns and rifles—mostly Enfield—killed and wounded not less than one hundred of the enemy, brought safely into camp two hundred horses and mules—besides remounting nearly the entire command—together with fifty-one prisoners, and about sixty negroes, who followed of their own accord.

Too much praise cannot be awarded Colonel Hatch for the skilful manner in which he handled his men against far superior numbers. His fight at Palo Alto—diverting the enemy from Colonel Grierson— did undoubtedly give the latter some thirty-six hours start of all incumbrances.

And now, while the command is resting, camped in the suburbs of Memphis, I will take the reader down to Wall's Bridge, Amit County, Mississippi, and tell what disposition was made of us who were left wounded at Mr. Newman's plantation, and with it bring my history of our journey to an end.

Conclusion

After receiving my wound I made my way back to the rear of the column, when with the assistance of a few comrades I was helped from my horse and laid upon the ground. They assisted me in changing my dress for that of the Federal army, and securing my side-arms, horse and equipments. I was then carefully laid into an ambulance, and conveyed to the plantation along with the rest of my wounded comrades. I remember of being carried through the front into a back room, joining the kitchen, and laid upon a pile of unginned cotton, which Hughes, Roy and myself occupied, the colonel remaining in the front room. I had not lain many minutes before it occurred to me, for the first time since receiving my wound, that I had considerable Confederate money in my possession, and acting on the impulse of the moment I concealed it by poking it down under the cotton, together with my pocket-knife, match-safe, and three dollars in silver and a breast-pin.

Shortly after this I heard considerable talking in the adjoining room—the one in which the colonel lay. The cause was soon explained, by seeing the doorway filled with Confederate soldiers. We excited some curiosity, and with few exceptions were treated with respect by them. Some threats were made against the colonel by a Confederate officer, who drew his sabre, threatening to plunge it through him. The colonel told him that he did not expect to live long, and as he had done nothing but his duty he would not ask for mercy at his hands. The Southern "chivalry" was prevented from putting his threat into execution by the timely interference of a superior officer, who reprimanded him severely. These soldiers proved to be the advance of Colonel Miles' command—better known in that region as Miles' Legion—having just arrived from Osyko Station, and in pursuit of Colonel Grierson.

I could plainly see the column from my window as it moved along. It consisted of about three hundred cavalry, two thousand infantry, and one battery of artillery—four and six pound rifled guns. They felt confident of capturing the "Yanks," and did not appear to be in any hurry, stating that a force had been sent out from Port Hudson, and that they would intercept our forces when they attempted to cross the Amit River.

Colonel Grierson had now five hours the start, and I knew that he would not let any grass grow under his feet. We were visited by the colonel while his command was passing. He informed us that he had instructed the nurses that they should pay every attention to the wounded. He treated us with kindness, and I shall never forget his kind manner and venerable form. He was afterwards captured at Port Hudson, and related his interview with Lieut.-Col. Blackburn, and the wounded men of our command, upon this occasion.

After they left I felt some anxiety about the command, fearing they would be cut off from crossing the river. Mr. Newman, the proprietor, had been pressed in by our command and taken as far as Greensburg. The women, being left alone, at first felt very much alarmed. Their fears were soon quieted by the arrival of some of their neighbours, who assisted them. They were all very kind, and did everything in their power to alleviate our sufferings. During the evening Mr. Wall, of Wall's Post Office, made his appearance, and evinced much desire to provide for our wants. He seemed to think we ought to have the assistance of a surgeon from Osyko Station, and without any delay started that evening on his mule, rode eleven miles, and returned that night, bringing with him an army surgeon, who displayed considerable skill in dressing the colonel's wounds. He had to leave the next morning, being ordered to Port Hudson, and would not receive any compensation for his trouble, saying that it was his duty, and his government paid him for his services.

Mr. Wall was another man of the same principles, but he complained bitterly, and regretted the loss of his saddle-horse, which our command had taken from his stable. It seemed to me that it was in my power to replace his loss by offering him the value of his horse in money. I felt influenced to act thus by the kindness and interest he had displayed in our welfare. Desiring to see him he was sent for. On his arrival I asked him how much he valued his horse at and he said five hundred dollars. I told him he should receive that amount for it—that it would be paid to him by Mrs. Newman. My reason for not paying him then was that I did not wish to show them where my money was concealed; no one had known of my having it except my comrades.

As the reader will want to know how much money I had, and how I came by it, I will explain. The amount was twenty-five hundred dollars, nearly all in Confederate fifty-dollar "graybacks," the remainder in notes of smaller dimensions. The money was handed to me by a member of the Seventh Illinois, who found it at Newton Station, floating on the water, as previously mentioned. The next morning, at about ten o'clock, Mr. Newman arrived, having been released by our command. It was a timely arrival, for many of the citizens were under the impression that he would be murdered, and had in circulation a rumour that our command had murdered Captain Scott, and many were the threats muttered against us, which they were prevented putting into execution by Mr. Wall, until the appearance of Mr. Newman, who, by his statement, dispelled all evil intentions. He also brought the joyful news that the command had safely crossed Amit River, which was confirmed a few hours later by the arrival of a courier, who was on his way to Osyko Station. He stated that the force sent out from Port Hudson consisted of two regiments of infantry and one battery of artillery, and when Colonel Grierson crossed the bridge the rebels were within five miles, waiting for daylight, so as to proceed—something Colonel Grierson did not wait to consult in cases of emergency. We all felt elated over the good news.

And now the question arose, what disposition would be made of us? We were all wounded in a manner that would not admit of our being moved. It was in the afternoon of the second day that a squad of cavalry arrived from Osyko Station, being sent as guard, with orders to bring us all to that place. They had a rickety old ambulance, which they intended to put us all into. Dr. Yole explained matters to them— that it was impossible to move any of the wounded except myself. After parleying awhile they submitted, and I was carried out and laid in the ambulance. As I was carried through the colonel's room I could not but notice how pale and haggard he looked. He was suffering intensely. I bid him goodbye, hoping that we would meet again.

Previous to leaving the room I saw Mrs. Newman, and having confidence in her I handed her twenty-three hundred dollars, my pin, miniature, pocket-knife and silver, keeping one hundred dollars myself. I requested her to pay Mr. Wall five hundred for his horse, and I would devise some way to get the balance. Dr. Yole, Le Sure and Douglas were ordered to accompany the escort on foot, which made them puff, on an eleven mile march, they not being used to infantry tactics. The colonel was left without any medical attendance, though every care and attention was bestowed on him by Mr. and Mrs. Newman.

About six o'clock we arrived at Osyko Station and halted in front of headquarters. I was surprised to hear and see the rebel Colonel Richardson, from Tennessee, who took particular delight in heaping abuse upon the Sixth and Seventh Cavalry, by saying everything that was mean and unbecoming a gentleman. He has since met with his reward, by being shot while attempting to make his escape from the Union forces. From this place I was moved to the depot, where I rested all night, very comfortably, on a cot. The next morning a soldier made his appearance, followed by a little girl, who carried a pitcher of coffee, some nice ham, biscuits, and tender beefsteak. It was really inviting, and my appetite being in a good condition I did ample justice to it. This soldier was actuated by a noble impulse. He had come voluntarily from his dwelling, and brought me a breakfast prepared by his wife. He had once been a prisoner, was taken at Fort Donelson, and was kindly treated by our army, and had not forgotten it. I am sorry that I have forgotten his name.

At an early hour I was put on board the train, on my way to Magnolia Station, ten miles north. Previous to starting I learned that the doctor and Le Sure were permitted to return to the colonel, on their parole, while Douglas was retained and would be sent to Richmond. On my way to Magnolia my boots and coat were stolen from beneath my cot. On my arrival at the latter place I was taken from the cars and carried to the hospital, up the first flight of stairs, and put into a large-sized room, in the north end of the building, fronting the street, on the east side of the railroad, with a *piazza* in front; the room was a very pleasant one. The building was built for a hotel, and used as such until the breaking out of this war. It was capable of accommodating about four hundred guests.

Connected with it was an extensive livery-stable, bowling saloon, billiard-rooms, bathing establishment, &c. Before the war this was a place of much resort from New Orleans, it being only ninety miles distant, and having a healthy location, surrounded by the beautiful magnolia trees in full bloom. A clear stream of water, abounding with fish, afforded sport for the angler. Magnolia Station did not contain more than two hundred buildings of all classes, a few stores, two hotels, and an extensive tannery, busily engaged manufacturing leather for the government.

I had not been here long before my wound was attended to by the principal surgeon, Dr. Huford, formerly from Baton Rouge, whom I found very kind in his treatment, but stern in his manner. He had some three hundred patients under his charge, and was assisted by Drs. Stebbling and Biggs, formerly of Kentucky. I shall never forget the kindness extended to me by those gentlemen. They would frequently visit my room, where I was alone, and sit and talk for hours at a time. This was very considerate in them, and a great privilege enjoyed by me. It was here I lay in suspense many a long hour, busy with thoughts of home and friends.

Contrary to what I anticipated I had not been searched, and was in possession of the following articles: one pair drawers, one pair overalls, one pair of socks, two shirts, and one hundred dollars in Confederate money—no hat, coat, boots, pants or jacket. The second day after my arrival my drawers, shirts and socks were washed, after which I felt quite comfortable. A black man was assigned to wait upon me, and I received every attention. The landlady—I have forgotten her name—furnished me with books to read, and occasionally would bring me in a fresh magnolia, which, placed in water, would keep the room sweet for several days.

Though the ladies of the South are to be admired for their graceful forms and manners, they indulge to excess in one habit—that of dipping snuff—which looks strange enough to Northern men. The hospital-steward was very kind, calling frequently to see me. My fare, though scant, was clean and properly cooked, which consisted of corn-bread, molasses, mush, sassafras tea, and almost invariably the leg of a goose for breakfast, baked, no dressing, sometimes tender as a spring chicken, then again tough enough to make a good whip-cracker; however my appetite was sufficient for all I could get. In the course of a week I was able to dress my own wound, by the aid of a glass, washing it every morning and evening with warm water and castile soap, keeping it constantly wet with cold water. I did not have occasion to take a single dose of medicine. The ball, in passing through my thigh, had just missed the main artery and bone, and the doctor said I would soon be able to go about on crutches.

I had permission to write a letter home, which the doctor told me would be forwarded through the lines, subject to military inspection. I felt rejoiced at this, and wrote a suitable letter, handed it to the doctor, and I supposed it was on its way and would soon be in the hands of my friends. I was doomed to disappointment. In a few days it was handed to me, with the unwelcome news that no more letters were allowed to pass the lines. I felt sad and lonely; this was my last and only hope of getting news home. My death had been published in the *Jackson Appeal*, and if one of those papers should get into our lines it would be copied, and my friends would think me dead. I was in suspense, but not forgetful of a kind Providence, that had spared me thus far. I put my trust in God, and tried to wait patiently.

In the meantime I was not forgetful of my wounded comrades, of whom I made daily inquiries—at one time hearing the colonel had died, the next it would be contradicted. It was impossible to get a correct story. Finally I succeeded, through the exertions of the steward, in hiring a man to go out to Mr. Newman's and learn the truth, at the same time to bring in a portion of my money. On the third day after leaving he returned, bringing the sad intelligence that after seventeen days of intense pain and suffering the colonel had died, also the man Hughes; that they were buried on the plantation, and that Roy, Le Sure and the doctor had reported to Osyko; that my property had been delivered over to Le Sure.

This was a sad disappointment to me. I feared I would not see my comrades again before they were sent to Richmond. Again the hospital-steward showed his kindness, by going on the train to Osyko Station and seeing the sergeant-major, who sent back word that he would pass next day, on his way to Richmond. I was now able to move around on crutches, and had been up and down stairs several times. The sergeant-major made his appearance next day, and handed me my breastpin and four hundred and fifty dollars, the balance of the twenty-three hundred which I left in the hands of Mrs. Newman. The five hundred had been paid to Mr. Wall, according to promise, and the remainder was used towards defraying the expenses of the wounded and nurses, burying the dead, &c., everything being scarce and consequently very expensive. It seemed as if the hand of Divine Providence directed the use of this money for this special purpose.

I was soon able to walk around, with the use of a cane, and was permitted to promenade the streets. I had a pair of shoes made, very common ones, for which I paid sixteen dollars. I also purchased some clothing, paying for a common felt hat thirty dollars, a light summer coat forty dollars, a pair of pants, half cotton, twenty dollars—cotton socks one dollar and thirty cents. I make mention of this that the reader may know how scarce and expensive articles were at that time in Dixie. The following prices were given me by the hospital-steward: flour one hundred and fifty dollars a barrel, none in market; coffee five dollars a pound, and a half a pound; eggs one dollar and a half a dozen; chickens, live, twelve dollars a dozen. The two first named articles I had not seen in the hospital.

I was now allowed the privilege of eating in the dining-room, with the non-commissioned officers, also of visiting the different wards. Among the patients I found one federal soldier, belonging to the navy. He had one leg amputated just below the knee. His name was William Hawkins. He served at one of the guns on the Indianola, when she was sunk by the rebel batteries at Port Hudson, where he received his wound and was taken prisoner. I found him a very intelligent person. We could sympathize with each other, were company for each other, and time passed more rapidly and agreeably.

It was very amusing sometimes to listen to the various reports respecting the army and battles, which, according to their statements, always resulted in their favour. There was a telegraph office at the depot which brought them daily news from Jackson, Mississippi. That, with the *Jackson Appeal*—which could tell the biggest lies, for a small paper, of any one published—were the only sources we had to obtain news. They took particular pains to report to me, which was very kind of them. At the time that Hooker withdrew from Fredericksburg, Virginia, they received the news that he lost forty thousand men in killed, wounded and prisoners, that he was completely routed, and his army flying in all directions.

A few days later and General Lee occupied Arlington Heights, and threatened to shell the city of Washington. The next report was that Grant had lost at Vicksburg, in storming the works, eighty thousand men, and owing to the excessive warm weather, and disgusting stench arising from the bodies, they had to be burned. They were confident of capturing his whole command, and had his supplies cut off. Following this was a report that Kirby Smith had crossed the Mississippi River, attacked Banks in the rear, and captured nearly all of his command; and lastly, that a Texas regiment of cavalry had met Colonel Grierson, wounded and taken him prisoner, together with nearly all of his command. You can imagine my feelings on hearing such reports. I could not contradict them, nor did I choose to believe all. I could; occasionally hear, after night, the reports of our mortars, as they were throwing their ponderous shells into Port Hudson, eighty miles distant.

I knew in that quarter, at all events, our forces still existed. Vicksburg was their boasted Gibraltar.

The month of May was now drawing to a close, and I was able to move around quite lively, feeling anxious to be sent North. My wishes were soon gratified. On the second day of June I was notified by the doctor that he would send me to Jackson on the morrow. I felt rejoiced at the thought of going towards home, and knowing that my friend Hawkins desired to accompany me I sought an interview with the doctor, and after considerable talking he consented to send him along, as I could be of some service towards assisting him. In the meantime I purchased two watches from inmates of the hospital, paying for them two hundred and fifty dollars. I thought this a good investment, knowing that the Confederate money would not be of any use inside of our lines.

The morrow came, and with it the train. At one o'clock Hawkins and myself went aboard, and were soon leaving Magnolia far in the rear, where I had remained just one month. Upon arriving at Summit Station I was told that we could not proceed further by railroad, as it had not been repaired since Grierson's command destroyed it. Here was a space of twenty miles which we must walk, or hire a private conveyance, paying fifteen dollars each. I at once procured passage for Hawkins, the Sergeant who was guarding us, and myself. It was here I again experienced the benefit of that money. After proceeding about half way we stopped at a house, where we stayed all night. We had not been here long before we were joined by other passengers.

I at once recognized the plantation and the proprietor as one on whom I had called with a squad of men, and taken two horses, while the command was destroying government property at Boyachitta, one mile distant. The planter did not recognize me, and I did not take the trouble to relate to him the circumstance. We were provided with a good bed and supper, for which I paid one dollar and fifty cents. The next morning at four o'clock we started for Brookhaven, arriving there at eight o'clock, just in time to take breakfast at the hotel before leaving on when we rode in so gallantly. The most familiar were those of the landlady and her daughter, at the hotel. I felt as though I would like to speak to them, but circumstances did not permit.

Aboard the train was an Englishman, who held a captain's commission in the rebel army. He amused me very much, not only by his foppish appearance, but by his ridiculous actions and the interest he took in watching me. I could not move but what he would tell the guard to keep his eyes on me. He belonged to that class of Englishmen who interfere with other people's business.

About one o'clock we arrived within two miles of Jackson. The train could not run further on account of the road being torn up by Sherman's forces, at the time they occupied the place. Here were quite a number of private conveyances. After obtaining one for my wounded friend I started for the city on foot with the sergeant. I had a very good opportunity of seeing the Capitol of the State, and was surprised to see so much of it left standing, having been told that our forces had destroyed the principal portion of it. The first place I was introduced to was the provost marshal's office, where I had to wait some two hours before being examined. While so doing I took occasion to hand Hawkins fifteen dollars, thinking he might need it, and we might be separated, which proved to be the case, he being examined and sent away the same evening, with a number of others, to Richmond. They allowed him to keep his money.

I bid him goodbye, not expecting to see him again. My turn came, and unfortunately for me, being neatly dressed, I was looked upon with suspicion, and ordered to strip myself to my shirt and drawers, which I did not hesitate to do. They then proceeded to search the pockets, lining, &c., appropriating to themselves my watches, papers, and all my money, except about twenty dollars, my pocket-knife and miniature pin, which they allowed me to keep—very considerate in them. I also had in my possession two letters from Doctors Stebbling and Biggs, which they requested me to mail after reaching our lines. They were not sealed, and contained nothing but what was of a domestic character. I felt sorry about those letters, for I had been kindly treated by those two gentlemen. The search ended, and they found nothing to implicate me. They expressed some disappointment in not finding any Lincoln greenbacks. I thought this rather queer proceedings for the head military authorities of Jackson.

I soon found I was not the only one subject to this treatment—others also suffered. The name of this specimen of "Southern chivalry," who appeared to be the star actor in this military drama, was J. C. Winnin. I think I will remember his face, and if I am ever so lucky as to meet him again will ask him the "time of day." From the provost marshal's office I was sent to the guard-house, a one and a half story frame house on Main street, where I lodged with about twenty-five others, and remained for thirty-six hours before receiving any rations, which, when they did come, consisted of a scanty supply of unsifted corn meal and refuse bacon—nothing else; no cooking utensils of any description, and nothing but cistern water to drink, on the top of which could be seen pieces of bacon floating.

I had not been here long before the lieutenant of the guard ordered me into a private room, and ordered me to undress, while he gave the garments a thorough examination. He found nothing. My pocket-knife seemed to please his fancy, which he kept, and it was only through my earnest entreaties that he allowed me to retain my miniature pin, for which I thanked him. The money he had no use for—greenbacks was what he was after. Among the prisoners were two citizens, who claimed to be residents of Memphis, Tennessee. They were very kind to me, inviting me to their table, which they had furnished from a hotel close by—a privilege not allowed soldiers.

Thus I fared very well, until the third day, when we were ordered to be in readiness to leave at nine o'clock next morning. At the appointed time we were found in line, twenty in all, and marched two miles, crossing the Pearl River, and taking the train on the Jackson and Mobile railroad were soon comfortably seated in a passenger car. Our guard consisted of one sergeant and six men—old soldiers—who treated us with kindness and respect. Before leaving Jackson we were not provided with rations, nor did we receive any until we arrived at Selma, Alabama.

The first place of any importance was Meridian, then the Tombigbee River, where we took a boat for Demopolis and again resumed the railroad, arriving at Selma the next afternoon. Remained all night, and received three day's rations of hard tack and boiled salt beef, (a very good article). We were kindly treated by the provost marshall, and looked upon with some curiosity by the citizens, as well as a show of sympathy and respect. Not being allowed the privilege of the streets I had no opportunity of viewing the place, but the small portion I could see impressed me favourably; the extensive buildings, fine roads, level sidewalks, shaded by beautiful trees, all looked neat and business like.

The greater portion of this State, through which we passed, appeared to be under good cultivation, and the crops looked very favourable. Corn appeared in abundance on all sides. The next morning we were marched down to the river, where we took deck passage on board a steamer for Montgomery, Ala. Before leaving Selma I saw what was said to be the keel of a boat on the stocks intended for a gunboat. One had been completed a short time before and launched. Our trip up the Alabama was very pleasant indeed; not being confined to close quarters, we enjoyed a fine view of its high banks, shaded by trees. In due time we arrived at the capitol of the State, where we remained a few hours. Taking the train we proceeded to West Point on the Alabama and Galine railroad, where we remained all night in a close building.

What little money I had upon leaving Jackson I had spent for something to eat, which I shared with some of my comrades who were in feeble health, two of whom belonged to the Fourteenth N.Y. Cavalry; our rations at this time becoming rather scant, I concluded to sell my coat, which I offered to the guard, for twenty-five dollars; he took it, at once paying the money. I derived more benefit from this money than I would have done by the use of my coat, by purchasing a few luxuries which benefited my health, and at the same time assisted my feeble companions who were not so fortunate as myself. The guards were very accommodating, allowing us many privileges. At an early hour next morning we left on a train arriving at Atlanta, Ga., where we were conducted to a guard house, a few blocks from the depot, at which place we had the pleasure of staying three days.

We were put into a small room in the second storey of a frame building which was surrounded by a high board fence, while several guards were patrolling their beats around us. Upon being put into this room I found it already occupied by about forty prisoners, the most of them citizens belonging to East Tennessee, who had been dragged from their homes and thrust into this filthy, loathsome room, because they loved the good old Union better than secession. It was a sorrowful sight to look upon the bent forms and wrinkled brows of these old men, whose heads were silvered by the frosts of seventy winters, and many were still older.

After living a life of honest industry, enjoying the privileges and blessings of a free and independent country, to be at last separated from wife and family by lawless hands and cast into a prison, there to subsist on a scant supply of corn bread and salt beef. For what? because they still continued to love the good old flag that had protected them so long. Our fare at this place consisted of a small piece of corn bread, about three inches square, twice a day, with a limited supply of salt-beef. Upon a table in the centre of the room (the only piece of furniture it contained,) stood a pail of water and one cup—this was the only drink we had.

Every man had been searched and every pocket-knife taken possession of by the jailor, a most brutal and unfeeling specimen of humanity. No one was permitted to look out of the window into the street; if he did violate this unreasonable order he ran the risk of being fired upon by the guard below, who was watching for the chance. One innocent citizen was shot dead a few days before our arrival for the above offence—the blood stains were still fresh on the window sill. From this place we were conducted to the depot by a new guard, where we took the train for Augusta.

As we left Atlanta I was surprised to see so many locomotives and cars; they were making this their depot for supplies for their army, which explained for the large amount of rolling-stock seen. I did within my heart wish that our cavalry could make a dash into this place and destroy this property.

Our trip through Georgia was not unpleasant considering our circumstances. The new guard were home guards, and were not very strict; and we were allowed to look out of the windows; so we had a good view of the country, and I noticed that wheat was the principal crop, which looked very well. On our arrival at Augusta, which was in the night, we changed cars, and just at daylight crossed the bridge over the Savannah River, a very pretty stream. We were now in South Carolina, and in due time we arrived at Columbus, the capitol of the State, through which we were marched, giving us a good opportunity of seeing a large portion of the business part of the city, as well as the suburbs. I must say it is a beautiful place, displaying good taste and abundance of wealth.

From this place we were conveyed in freight box-cars, which at that time I thought very cruel, (but since have experienced the same treatment in my adopted State of Illinois, from Alton to Springfield, when returning home on furlough, as a veteran, with the regiment to which I belonged, after serving my country two years and eight months,) I came to the conclusion it was not so bad after all. From Columbus we went direct to Chesterville, soon passing out of the hot bed of secessionism. This was the only State we passed through that we received any taunts from the citizens, many of whom seemed to take delight in spitting their venom upon us.

On one occasion they remarked how meanly we were dressed; that there was no uniformity about our clothes; and I took pains to tell them the cause—that when taken prisoners our captors made an exchange with us—our boots, pants, hats, and sometimes our coats or jackets; thus the cause of our appearing so ragged and offensive. This did not sit well, and some of them were for breaking the d——d Yankee heads. The crops in this State did not look so well as through

Alabama and Georgia, though we passed through some very delightful country.

The first place of any importance we arrived at in North Carolina was Charlotte, thence to Salisbury, Greensboro, Raleigh, Goldsboro and Weldon, the last place bordering close upon Va, and fortified to some extent, though few troops were stationed there at that time. Our trip through this State was not unpleasant. The country through which we passed was not prepossessing in appearance. One incident occurred while passing through this State worthy of note. While stopping at a wood station to wood up, I saw an individual approaching our car, who, as soon as he came up, inquired, in North Carolina accent, if any of us had Confederate money we wished to exchange for Lincoln greenbacks. I inquired how much he had. He replied five dollars, and would give it for five dollars in Confederate money; that he had carried the d——d abolition money long enough, and nobody wanted it out here.

I hauled out my pile, amounting to eight dollars, and handing him five received the greenback, which looked natural enough, and made one feel sort of good. The question arose in my mind, how will I keep it hid from the searching eyes of the Richmond officials. We had been informed by the guard that we would all be strictly searched and examined immediately on our arrival at Libby prison. An idea occurred to me how I might save my greenback, which I put into execution. I had remaining, tied up in an old dirty handkerchief, a few hard biscuits that I had bought. I borrowed a knife of one of the guard, and unperceived by them I cut a square piece out of the side of one of the biscuits, and scooping a hole out in the centre large enough I concealed my money together with my miniature pin; plugging up the hole again, I took care not to break into those biscuits which were hard and dirty.

On our arrival at Petersburg we were delayed a few hours, and then, "On to Richmond," nineteen miles distant. When about half way between those two places we came in sight of the rebel fortifications, which are expected to protect Richmond. The works are very extensive, extending some eight or ten miles, and two to five miles in breadth, and, if well defended, will take an immense army and hard fighting to get possession of.

I will here take occasion to make some remarks respecting their railroads. Those over which I passed, as a general thing, were pretty well used up—track very rough, and rolling stock out of repair. They could not average more than fourteen miles per hour. The most substantial track was in South Carolina. On the afternoon of the fourteenth of June we arrived at the capitol of the Southern Confederacy, being ten days on our way from Jackson, Miss. We were marched down through the main street where every idle spectator could gaze at us, which we returned in full.

We were soon introduced to that hospitable mansion, "Libby Prison," so familiar to so many of our brave boys; and where, by close confinement and cruel treatment, many a brave heart has beat its last within its walls, whose spirit gone forth to a just God will be avenged. We were formed in line fronting the prison, and almost the first man I saw was Sergt.-Major Le Sure, and the next, Dr. Yole. I felt pleased at seeing my old companions and longed to speak to them, which was not permitted just then. We were ordered into the building, and formed in line through a narrow hall, when the search commenced, passing through the entire line, finding but little plunder beside canteens and haversacks—the two latter they invariably kept.

Upon presenting my biscuits they were looked upon with contempt. I felt satisfied with the result and still continued to freeze to them. The next proceeding was to take our names, rank, number of regiment to which we belonged, what State, &c. We were then paroled, signed an article of agreement, and swore not to do so and so until duly and lawfully exchanged. After this, we were told the joyful news that we should be sent away to City Point with a batch that was to start in the morning; for this, I felt really thankful. From the hall we were conducted to another apartment, up two flights of stairs, into a large room crowded with Union soldiers.

The first thing we heard upon entering was the cry of "fish, fish, more fish;" at first I could not imagine what it meant; I thought they were receiving rations, and I began to anticipate something good to eat; imagine my disappointment when I discovered that we were the object of all this noise and confusion. The prisoners had adopted a rule—that of keeping a man on sentry at the stairway and when any new prisoners arrived to cry out "fish, fish," which sentence would be taken up and repeated by nearly everyone in the room, while they would flock to the stairway, expecting to see some old friends and comrades.

The size of this room was sixty by forty feet, with no ventilation except what came from three heavily barred windows at each end. It contained no article of furniture whatever, and was crowded with about three hundred and forty men. At the lower end, and about the centre was a small closet, six by four feet, in which a pipe entered coming up from the canal below; this afforded drinking water, as well as wash room and water closet. You may well blush, but such are facts. Picture to yourself this room at night, the floor covered with human frames, inhaling such impure air. The stench that then arose was almost suffocating, enough to cause disease and sickness.

Besides the soldiers there was other company, and plenty of it, well known by the name of "graybacks" in the army. Our rations consisted of a limited supply of flour bread, a small piece of boiled salt beef, and a mixture called Confederate coffee, which was anything but agreeable to the taste or appearance. Before retiring that night we were notified that we would start next morning at three o'clock and for every man to be awake and ready, that no one would be permitted to take his blanket with him. I laid down, not to sleep, but to think of Libby Prison, and how thankful I should feel that a kind Providence had favoured me thus far; then I pictured home and all its inmates, who were anxiously waiting to hear some word or news concerning me; perhaps they thought me dead, if so, what a sweet disappointment my presence would create; and thus, I fancied in thought until sleep closed my eyes.

At an early hour next morning everybody appeared to be awake; all was excitement and confusion, but we did not have to wait long before a guard appeared at the stairway and gave the order to move out until we reached the street and then form fours. We soon arrived at the depot, some five hundred in all, taking the cars to Petersburg, then changing and making a short run we were soon at City Point. I perceived there were no officers aboard, and upon inquiry, was told that they would not be exchanged for a long time. I felt sorry for them, and was glad that I was not an officer. While waiting at Petersburg a few hours I saw several strangers in a sly way offering four dollars in Confederate money for one in greenbacks.

Upon reaching City Point, toward the neutral ground for exchange of prisoners, our sight was greeted by the old flag, whose stars and stripes were floating defiantly and proudly from the mast-head of the steamer New York. Cheer after cheer rent the air, and tears could be seen trickling down the cheeks of more than one brave hero, whose heart was full to the brim with gladness at once more beholding the emblem of liberty.

Like the symbol of love and redemption its form,
As it points to the haven of hope, and the nation;
How radiant each star, as the beacon afar,
Gives promise of peace or assurance of war.
How peaceful and blest was America's soil
Till betrayed by the guile of the traitor demon,
Who lurks under virtue, and springs from his coil,
To fasten his fangs on the life-blood of freedmen;
Then boldly appeal to each heart that can feel,
And the flag of our country shall in triumph remain,
To guide us to victory and glory again.

From the cars we all rushed to the river, and after taking a good wash in its bright waters, feeling much refreshed, were ordered to form twos and march aboard of Uncle Sam's boat, and as we stepped upon its clean white deck the first thing that we saw, which was served out to us, was a large slice of fresh bread and boiled ham, and a large tin-cup full of real old Java coffee. Wasn't it good? If you doubt it, just ask any soldier who has been in Libby Prison until half starved. Who would not fight for such a government as we possess? What a contrast! Just view the picture. There are landed at this very spot three or four hundred Confederate prisoners, fresh from a Northern prison. They look clean, healthy and strong, are well dressed; each man is in possession of a blanket, and a haversack, which is filled with good rations; he is fully prepared to enter immediately into active service.

On the other hand here comes a few hundred Union prisoners, fresh from Libby Prison or Bell Island; their garments are ragged and dirty—robbed of their own clothes, they receive old garments of every description—their steps are weak and tottering—their forms are wasted away to mere skeletons—their spirits broken. They are no longer fit subjects for the battlefield—close confinement in a filthy room and starvation has brought them to this condition. They carry no blankets, haversacks or rations. This is Southern chivalry, Southern hospitality—and as the war is prolonged the more barbarous is the treatment inflicted upon their prisoners. The inmates of Libby Prison, the inmates of Bell Island, God help them! they deserve the pity and sympathy of all Christians.

As we left City Point I bade farewell to Southern hospitality. I have no desire to taste its sweets again. As we glide swiftly down the stream how refreshing the breeze! how sweet is liberty! We were allowed to range over the boat at pleasure, which was guarded by a portion of the few that remained of the famous Ninth New York Volunteers—Hawkins' Zouaves—a noble, manly set of men, neat in attire and perfect in discipline. They treated us with every kindness, particularly M. E. and J. L. Fitzgerald, company K. The officers of the boat were also unremitting in their attentions.

The scenery along the James River presents some beautiful landscape views. As we came in sight of Fortress Monroe we could see our gunboats—the two extremes, the old man-of-war *Constitution*, three decker, carrying—guns, and nearby could be seen the little iron-plated *Monitor*, apparently not more than twelve inches above the water, with a round turret, carrying two ponderous guns. As we came opposite the fort the boat anchored and a yawl was lowered, which conveyed the captain to the fort to report to the commander of the post.

While lying here I could see at a distance the immense Lincoln Gun, capable of throwing a one hundred pound shot six miles with great accuracy. Who would have believed it twenty years ago? In the meantime I had not forgotten my biscuit, and cut it open in the presence of a gaping crowd, who looked with perfect astonishment when they beheld the pin and greenbacks extracted. They allowed it was genuine sleight of hand. After a few hours delay the order was given to weigh anchor, and with steam up we started for Annapolis, Maryland, arriving there the next afternoon in time to march up to the camp of parole.

We were formed in close column and ordered by the major commanding for each man to answer to his name as it was called, and he would assign troops from different states each one by themselves; this being accomplished a short address was made by the major, stating that those who desired clothing to report to the quartermaster department and they would be furnished it, also a quantity of soap, and every member was advised to visit the bay close by, where they could indulge in a salt-water bath. I assure you there was some scrubbing done just about that time, after which a new suit of clothing throughout was put on, which made us look once more respectable. Of rations we had plenty and good, and were allowed the limits of the town as long as we did not abuse the privilege. It was quite refreshing to visit the oyster stands down near the water's edge; and indulge in some fresh from their native brine.

Annapolis is the capital of the State, a delightful location, surrounded by beautiful scenery. A very extensive Naval Academy is established here, but since the war broke out the buildings are used as hospitals. A more appropriate place could not be selected. The streets present a very odd appearance, radiating from the State House. A large number of the buildings are of the old style of architecture, and the old State House still remains, in which Washington used to give to the world his noble sentiments.

Among the many soldiers that were here on our arrival I was pleased to find some of my old comrades—Sergeant Vaughn, who accidentally wounded himself near Union Church, Corporal Douglass, from Osyka, and friend Hawkins. After remaining here about ten days an order was read at roll-call for all Western troops to be in readiness, at an early hour next morning, to take the road for Baltimore. Starting at the time appointed we crossed Chesapeake Bay, having a very pleasant trip. It was amusing to watch the schools of porpoises roll leisurely over and then disappear. It was about two o'clock when we arrived in Baltimore, and at once marched up to the Soldiers' Association Hall, where a good table was supplied for us, and lodgings for the night. The next morning we left by train on the Pennsylvania Central Railroad, over a good track, making excellent time. We soon found ourselves winding around the hills, through ravines, woodlands, and over streams, with mountain peaks in the distance, which we were fast approaching.

And oh! how the heart did beat with joy to witness at almost every house the waving of handkerchiefs and star spangled banners. It was one continual display of patriotism. To me it was the first demonstration of the kind I had seen for fifteen months. The next day we arrived at Pittsburg, Pennsylvania, after a pleasant ride through a fine agricultural country, presenting a variety of beautiful scenery, where we were conducted to Union Hall and partook of a sumptuous dinner, served by the fairest daughters of Pittsburg. From here we proceeded in separate parties, those belonging to the Army of the Cumberland being sent to Camp Chase, Ohio, and those belonging to the Mississippi department being sent to Bentoa Barracks, St. Louis, Missouri.

After arriving in Illinois I soon discovered that the train would pass within ten miles of my home. I had been absent about two years. The temptation was so strong that I naturally dropped off, and in a few hours afterwards was joyfully received by my friends. I immediately reported by letter to the commanding officer at Benton Barracks, and by keeping a strict watch I received the first notice through the public prints of an exchange, and at once started for Memphis, Tennessee, joining my regiment at Colliersville, on the C. and M. Railroad, October 13th, 1863, after an absence of five months and thirteen days. There was a general greeting of old friends, particularly with the scouts, who I found occupying the same position they held previous to the raid. They had met with no reward, and it was some time before I was permitted to resume my former duties; but regardless of position let all who love freedom, justice, and their country,

Strike for the Union! let her name ever be
The boast of the true and the brave;
Let freedom's bright star still shine on her brow,
And her banner the proudest to wave.
Strike for the Union! shall the heroes that fell
In graves all unhonoured repose,
While the turf on each head and the sword by each side
Has been stained by the blood of the foes?

Chorus.—*Three cheers for our land of the free,*
Three cheers for our noble and true,
For freedom, right, and liberty,
Our flag of the Red, White and Blue.

Strike for the Union! for liberty's sun
In darkness and gloom has not set;
Her bright beams still shine, like a light from above,
And will lead thee to victory yet.
Strike for the Union! for her weapons are bright,
And the heroes who wield them are strong;
Let her name brightly glow on the record of time,
And hers be the proudest in song.

Chorus.—*Three cheers for our land of the free.*

Strike for the Union! we will honour her name,
For the glorious deeds she has done;
The laurel will twine on each patriot's brow,
And shout when the battle is won.
Strike for the Union! it must never be said
That her banner was furled to a foe;
Let those stars ever shine in bright glory above,
And the pathway to victory show.

Chorus.—*Three cheers for our land of the free.*

The following is a roster of the officers of the Sixth and Seventh

Illinois Cavalry regiments, on their arrival at Baton Rouge, May 2nd, 1863:

SIXTH.

Field and Staff.
Col. B. H. Grierson, commanding.
Lieut.-Colonel, B. Loomis.
First Major, M. H. Starr.
Third Major, C. W. Whitsit.
Assistant-Surgeon, A. B. Agnew.

Non-Commissioned Staff.
Sergeant-Major, D. S. Flagg.
Q. M. Sergeant, T. Legget.
Com.-Serg't, Wm. Pollard.

First Battalion.
Captain A. D. Prince, Co. A.
Captain W. W. Patterson, Co. B.
Captain D. Angley, Co. C.
First-Lieut. Chas. Howard, Co. C.
Captain I. Conn, Co. D.
First-Lieut. H. Daily, Co. D.
Second-Lieut. L. V. Allen, Co. D.

Second Battalion.
Captain John Lynch, Co. E.
First- Lieut. E. Ball, Co. E.
Second-Lt. H. W. Stewart, Co. E.
Captain G. W. Sloan, Co. F.
First-Lieut. W. H. Dove, Co. F.
Second-Lt, G. W. Newell, Co. F.
Captain W. D. Glass, Co. G.
Second-Lt. S. L. Woodward, A.A.
Captain S. L. Marshall, Co. H.
First-Lieut. D. Manling, Co. H.

Third Battalion.
Captain L. B. Skinner, Co. I.
Second-Lt. D. L. Grimes, Co. H.
Captain F. Charlesworth, Co. L.
Second-Lt. J. W. Hughes, Co. L.

Seventh.

Field And Staff.

Col. Ed ward Prince, commanding.

Adjutant, George W. Root.

Non-Commissioned Staff.

Veter'y Surg'n, A. G. Levering.

Hospital Steward, Charles Hall.

First Battalion.

Captain Charles Hunting, Co. A.

First-Lt. J. J. La Grange, Co. A.

Second-Lt. D.V. Rhea, Co. A.

Captain G. W. Trafton, Co G.

First-Lieut. J. Gaston, Co. G.

Second-Lt. Wm. Stiles, Co. G.

Captain W. H. Reynolds, Co. D.

First-Lt. D. W. Bradshaw, Co. D.

Captain J. K. Fleming, Co. K.

First-Lt. J. W. Maxwell, Co. K.

Second Battalion.

Captain William Ashmead, Co. I.

Sec'd-Lt. S. H. Richardson, Co. C.

Captain I. M. Graham, Co. E.

First-Lieut. N. G. Wiley, Co. E.

Second-Lt. I. M. Caldwell, Co. E.

Captain S. A. Epperson, Co. L.

First-Lieut. W. W. Porter, Co. L.

Third Battalion.

Captain A. W. McDonald, Co. F.

First-Lieut. C. F. Lew, Co. F.

Second-Lt. James Breze, Co. F.

Captain B. C. F. Johnson, Co. M.

First-Lieut. Charles Stall, Co. M.

Second-Lieut. Henry Nicholson.

Capt. Milton L. Webster, Co. H.

Second-Lieut. S. A. Kitch, Co. H.

Captain Henry Forbes, Co. B.

First-Lieut. William McCausland.

Second-Lieut. Jos. O. Ram, Co. B.

Charles Hall, hospital-steward, was the only medical attendant of the Seventh Illinois that accompanied the expedition, and he deserves much praise for his unremitting care and attention to the wants of the suffering during the raid and while at Baton Rouge.

Brevet Maj.-Gen. Hatch.

Hatch's Sixty-Four Days' March

By order of Maj.-Gen. Washburne, commanding the Department of West Tennessee, Brig.-Gen. Edward Hatch, commanding first division cavalry corps, was ordered to hold his command in readiness to march, with ten days rations, and, if possible, form a junction with the United States forces then operating up the Tennessee River, as far as Eastport, Miss. The division was composed of the following troops: The first brigade, commanded by Colonel Oliver Wells, Twelfth Missouri Cavalry, and consisting of the Seventh and Third Illinois and Twelfth Missouri cavalry regiments; the second brigade, commanded by Colonel Datus E. Coon, Second Iowa Cavalry, consisting of the Sixth and Ninth Illinois and Second Iowa Cavalry, and company K, .First Illinois Light Artillery, Captain J. W. Curtis, commanding, the whole numbering about twenty-four hundred men, rank and file. The expedition was fitted out at White Station, on the line of the Memphis and Charleston Railroad, within seven miles of Memphis, Tennessee.

September 30th, 1864. The column moved out on the Germantown road; the rain fell in torrents for two hours. When within one mile of Germantown they turned north and crossed Wolf River, at Pattine's plantation; the crossing was upon a poorly constructed bridge, which delayed the wagons and artillery until after dark, and caused much trouble in passing through the heavily timbered bottom on the opposite side. The command was in bivouac by eleven o clock, seven miles north of Germantown.

October 1st. Left camp at daylight, the first brigade in the advance passed through Macon at 12 o'clock, and took the Sommerville road, camping three miles from the former place.

October 2nd. Moved out of camp at four o'clock, reached Sommerville and took the Boliver road, arriving at that place at four o'clock p.m. Here a heavy detail from the Second Iowa was sent to assist the Seventh Illinois in constructing a bridge across the Hatchie River— they were sent six hours in advance the evening previous. At eight o'clock, a.m., the bridge was completed, and the whole command crossed over and went into camp, except the Seventh Illinois, which did not cross until the next morning.

October 3rd. Moved out of the Hatchie bottom at daylight, taking the Mt. Pincton road, southeast of Jackson, crossed the Forkadeer River at sunset, and camped at eight o'clock in a heavy rain.

October 4th. Left camp at three o'clock, a.m., and reached Miffin, Henderson County, fed horses, prepared coffee and rations, and moved at ten o'clock, taking the road leading down the valley of Beach River, leaving Lexington to our left and north some eight miles. Camped at Jones' plantation, three miles from Scott's Hill; rained all day.

October 5th. Moved at daylight, passing Scott's Hill, taking the Decaturville road, at which place we arrived at two o'clock, P.M., and halted one hour to feed. At sunset reached the Tennessee River, opposite Clifton, Hardin County, having crossed a very impracticable, rocky, picturesque country. At Clifton we found the gunboat fleet and transports, under command of Maj.-Gen. C. C. Washburne.

October 6th. Arrangements were made early this morning to cross the river, by means of the *transports City of Pekin, Kenton* and *Aurora.* At two o'clock the command was all over, and in accordance with orders from Brig.-Gen. Hatch it moved out in direction of Waynesboro, on the Nashville pike, for twelve miles, and camped for the night on a beautiful hillside.

October 7th. We left camp at an early hour, moving towards Waynesboro, passing through that little place at ten o'clock, a.m., which is the county-seat. The command stopped and fed on the plantation of Mr. W. C. Barnes, a very respectable man. Waynesboro is 41 miles from Florence, 44 miles from Pulaski, and 92 miles from Nashville. The country is mountainous, rugged and barren, covered with vast and unknown forests, and filled with beautiful trout streams, whose clear waters gleam like pearls in their rocky basins. It is not very thickly settled, owing to its sterility. The roads being in good condition we made good time, and camped within seven miles of Lawrenceburg.

October 8th. Resumed our march this morning at three o'clock,

BREVET BRIG.-GEN. COON.

amid the most intense darkness. We took the wrong road and were led some five miles out of the way. We halted at nine o'clock for breakfast and to feed. Reached Lawrenceburg, the county-seat of Lawrence County, at one o'clock—a dilapidated, ancient looking place, and after a short rest moved out on military road leading to Florence, Alabama. When three miles out we took the road leading down the valley of Shoal Creek, through the most picturesque of countries, and camped for the night on its bank, ten miles from Lawrenceburg.

October 9th. Left this encampment at daylight, returning to the military road, and moving in the direction of Florence. Reached Baugh's Mills, and received orders to camp for the night. At this place we learned that Forrest had crossed the Tennessee River and escaped unharmed.

October 10th. At four o'clock this morning we were again in motion. On arriving at Wilson's crossroads we changed our course and moved toward Waterloo, passing to the north of Florence some six miles. We reached Waterloo at four o'clock, p.m., and camped.

October 11th. Remained in camp until four o'clock, p.m., when the command moved down the river some ten miles, with the hope of finding the gunboats and fleet, and procuring rations for the men. To make this more certain Major C. C. Horton, commanding the Second Iowa, was sent in advance with his regiment to the fleet with dispatches. Unfortunately the fleet had left a few hours previous to the arrival of our cavalry opposite Eastport, Miss.

October 12th. The command left camp at four o'clock, a.m., moving in the direction of Savannah, and at two o'clock, p.m., was snugly encamped one mile below that place.

October 13th. There being no visible signs of procuring rations for the command, who had been subsisting on the country at a poor rate some three days, we still remained in camp. Brigade commanders applied to General Hatch, who gave them permission to send out detachments of men, under suitable officers, and procure corn and wheat and have it ground at the neighbouring mills. This supplied a scanty amount for the next four days.

October 14th, 15th and 16th. During this time each day was industriously spent at the mills, by parties grinding wheat and corn, while others scoured the country to procure bacon, salt, &c., to make it palatable. In great anxiety they waited for the boats, until the evening of the 16th, when orders were received to move in the morning.

October 17th. At seven o'clock, a.m., we moved out on the Waynesboro road a distance of some ten miles, when we turned toward Clifton, at which place we camped, having marched thirty miles, over a very rough road, and having to forage off the country, which is a very disagreeable necessity, and cuts both friends and foes most cruelly.

October 18th. On arriving at Clifton no boats were in sight. The "grand rounds," on a large scale—some 150 miles—had been made, and we returned to the starting point, very hungry, ragged, and tired. During the afternoon, while unwelcome feelings were causing us to cast about for some means of subsistence, the steamer *Duke* came in sight, to the great satisfaction of the whole command. Our fine hopes were soon blasted, for we learned that it only had short rations of hard-bread and meat, which was equally distributed among the different regiments, the balance to be gathered from the country, during the absence of the steamer to Johnsonville.

From the 18th to the 27th of the month the officers and men were industriously employed in shoeing horses, and making necessary preparations for an active campaign. Owing to the scarcity of blacksmiths and tools scouting parties were sent out in the country to press in sufficient to supply the deficiency. Only a few were obtained, and many horses were shod by the use of the common pocket-knife and a hatchet. The horses improved, as forage was abundant.

While camped at Clifton, Tennessee, it was not an unusual occurrence for the rebels to make their appearance on the opposite side for the first few days, and considerable sharp-shooting was practiced by the men. At last both parties entered into an agreement not to fire upon each other, and a lively conversation ensued between them across the stream. Taking advantage of circumstances, Major Graham and Dr. Briggs, both of the Seventh Illinois Cavalry, procured an old canoe, hallooed over to them, asking if they would receive company. The rebels assented, and promised not to fire upon them, or detain them. Away they went, and upon landing were greeted by the "Johnnies" most cordially, who appreciated the visit highly, complimenting the major and doctor, and more particularly the good old Bourbon, a bottle of which the doctor presented to them.

Among the rebels was a surgeon by the name of Green, belonging to a Texas regiment, with whom the visitors had a very lively and agreeable conversation. The surgeon, on receiving the bottle, mounted himself upon a stump, and attracting the attention of the men on the opposite side, displayed the bottle and hallooed across to them to give three cheers for Old Abe, which was heartily responded to; then turning to his visitors drank to the success of Old Abe, (a remarkable circumstance, but true,) after which the parties returned, much pleased with their visit, the main object of which was to obtain information respecting three soldiers belonging to the Third Illinois Cavalry, who had been sent down the river in a skiff, some ten days previous, to ascertain the whereabouts of the gunboats. Their not reporting to their command in a reasonable length of time led to the supposition that they had been captured by the enemy. No information was gained concerning them.

October 29th. Left Clifton at three o'clock, p.m., taking the Nashville pike. Camped three miles out.

October 30th. At nine o'clock we moved towards Waynesboro, as far as Lincoln Creek, twenty-four miles from Clifton, and camped.

October 31st. Resumed the march this morning, reached Lawrenceburg, and camped one mile beyond.

November 1st. Left camp at six o'clock, a.m., and reached Pulaski, eighteen miles distant, and camped for the night.

November 2nd, 3rd and 4th. During these three days the time was occupied in procuring clothing and rations for the men, while shoes were being fitted on the horses, and preparations made for a heavy campaign. On our arriving at Pulaski we found two divisions of the Fourth Army Corps, under command of Maj.-Gen. Stanley. General Croxton's cavalry command was below, toward Florence. While here a brigade of cavalry arrived, consisting of the Fourteenth and Sixteenth Illinois and the Eighth Kentucky regiments. The Twenty-Third Army Corps, commanded by Maj.-Gen. Schofield, was reported to be *en route* for this place. Railroad trains arrived daily from Nashville, bringing supplies.

November 5th. Left camp with three days rations, marching from Pulaski southwest toward Florence. We were joined there by General Croxton's command, who were ordered to report to General Hatch. Our forces were reported to be at Shoal Creek, where the enemy was also reported to sustain his pickets. During the afternoon of this day heavy cannonading was heard in the direction of the Tennessee River, which gave undoubted evidence of Hood's advance into Tennessee. The command camped for the night on Sugar Creek. A beautiful sunset was witnessed, for the first time in three days, it having rained constantly. This gave the men more life, and raised their drooping spirits.

November 6th. Pushing out of camp before daylight enabled us to reach Lexington, Ala., before eleven o'clock, a.m., where we halted for an hour, to learn the movements of the enemy. Getting no reliable information the command moved on to Baugh's Ford, on Shoal Creek, the Second Iowa Cavalry in advance. On arriving within two miles of the ford the advance met the enemy's pickets, driving them across the creek rapidly, when the whole command came in full view of a heavy line, extending along the bluff on the opposite side. By order of General Hatch a detachment of the Second Iowa, under Lieutenant George W. Budd, commanding company G, was sent for the purpose of destroying by fire a flouring mill, which was located above a factory.

After a lively skirmish of nearly an hour the lieutenant returned and reported that the mill was on the opposite side of the stream, and that the water was too high to admit of crossing, mounted or dismounted—besides the enemy were some three hundred strong, and a large number posted in and about the mill, rendering the position almost impregnable, to say nothing of the difficulty of crossing the stream. On learning these facts the general directed a withdrawal of the whole command, except the Second Iowa, which was sent to remain and hold its position until further orders. At 9 o'clock, p.m., the command went into camp, in a most unpleasant rain storm.

November 7th. Daylight found us with mud and water under foot, and a drenching rain still falling. Information obtained stated that Hood's forces were located between here and Florence. The Second Iowa was withdrawn to feed. At one o'clock Colonel Coon was ordered to take his brigade and make a demonstration upon the enemy's pickets, the Ninth Illinois, Captain Wm. C. Blackburn, commanding, in advance. A persistent and heavy skirmish took place, when the enemy were driven from the bluff on the opposite side. The regiment reached the ford, but the creek was too much swollen to admit of crossing, the water carrying horse and rider down the stream. During an hour spent in skirmishing, and an unfruitful effort to cross and destroy the mill, it was ascertained beyond doubt that the enemy had reinforced the pickets heavily, and that Shoal Creek was much higher than at any day previous. The second brigade was withdrawn, falling back to Slutt's Cross-Roads, and camped for the night. It had rained all day.

November 8th. The whole command remained in camp this day, with exception of detachments sent out to reconnoitre, &c. This afforded the men an opportunity to vote for President, the result of which was that an overwhelming majority was given for "Honest Old Abe." At two o'clock, p.m., the detachments sent out in the morning returned. They all reported, as the three days previous, that the stream could not be forded. An effort was made by the Second Iowa to construct a raft to cross to the mill, but failed for want of material. During a skirmish of an hour the rain fell in torrents, and soon night came on, closing all operations for the day. The second brigade was withdrawn to a point near the bivouac of the previous night. Major C. C. Moore, Second Iowa, was immediately sent out, with a detachment of one hundred men, to the rear of the enemy on the Tennessee River, with instructions to strike the river ten miles below Florence.

November 9th. During the night Colonel Coon received orders from General Hatch to move out early in the morning with his brigade, and make another demonstration on the enemy at Baugh's Ford. At nine o'clock the ford was reached; the road was nearly impassable from mud and water. They found the enemy's pickets heavy and well posted on the opposite side—the stream still too high to admit of fording from either side. The brigade withdrew during the afternoon and camped at Wadkin's House. It rained nearly all day, but cleared away at sunset. In the meantime Major Moore, Second Iowa, returned with his command safe, having passed around in rear of the enemy's line, a distance of forty miles, and striking the Tennessee River ten miles below Florence, making a distance, in going and returning, of eighty miles travel in twenty-four hours. The object of this expedition was to bring in some men of General Croxton's command, who had been three days previously sent down the river from Bainbridge to destroy the enemy's pontoons at Florence, which was not accomplished. They were to complete the work of destruction and meet this party below, but after diligent search and careful inquiry the Major returned.

November 10th. Remained in camp all day, the first pleasant day since leaving Pulaski. Owing to the very inclement weather, bad roads, &c., the whole command was again entirely destitute of rations. Two mills were taken possession of, and a regular system of foraging off the country was adopted, which, with the most careful management, could but poorly supply the men. Orders were given for the whole command to be ready to move upon the enemy next morning.

November 11th. The division moved out, the second brigade advancing on the Baugh's Ferry road, the remainder of the force moving on the Huntsville, Bainbridge and military roads. It was not long before each command was engaged, skirmishing with the enemy's pickets. The Sixth Illinois, Major Chas. C. Whitrish, commanding, had the advance of the second brigade, and were deployed as skirmishers, dismounted, forming a line from the main road up the stream to the mill, while a section of artillery was put in position on the military road. The skirmishers soon drove back their pickets, while the artillery caused their reserve, at first in plain sight, to scatter to the rear. A company of mounted men were, in the meantime, to try the ford on the main road and ascertain its condition for crossing.

After a thorough trial it was found too deep, even for mounted men. The Second Iowa, Major C. C. Horton, commanding, succeeded in finding a crossing, nearly one-fourth of a mile below the main crossing. Col. Coon dispatched an orderly to the major for him to cross as rapidly as possible, which order was obeyed, in a most gallant manner, by company G, of that regiment, with Lieutenant Geo. W. Budd commanding, in the advance. The first battalion, Major Gustavus Schwitgar commanding, was soon over and engaging the enemy in a brisk skirmish, when Major Horton reported the ford impracticable for the passage of more troops, owing to the quicksand and miry soil on the opposite shore, and that it was impossible to cross the artillery in any event. The major was ordered to dismount the remainder of his regiment, place them in line along the shore, and recall Major Schwitgar.

In crossing and re-crossing the stream the enemy kept up a heavy fire from a barricade some three hundred yards distant, on a high bluff. Another effort was made to cross at the mill, but failed. The Ninth Illinois Cavalry, Capt. Blackburn commanding, had been sent, on leaving camp, to make a flank movement to the right of their position, by crossing Shoal Creek above the pond and mill, and moving down on the opposite and west side of the stream. They now appeared in sight, fighting the enemy's pickets to such an extent that they fell back so far that the Second Iowa was enabled to cross by swimming their horses, which feat was accomplished in safety, with one exception— Lieutenant David Hilliars, commanding company A, who, by a misunderstanding of orders, took the wrong track, and being sorely pressed by a brigade of the enemy's cavalry, coolly took to the timber and hills, evading their main force, and after much difficulty succeeded in re-crossing Shoal Creek, and reporting with all his men in camp at dark. The cool, undisturbed manner of this officer in releasing himself from the snare of the enemy is at least highly complimentary. This evening the command camped again at Wadkin's House.

November 12th. Remained in camp all day. Issued a very light ration of meal ground at the mills.

November 13th. Remained in camp all day. Orders were received from General Hatch for the brigade to send heavy details to all the fords and main roads, and by felling timber to obstruct the passage of the enemy. This was done to enable the command to shift from right to left, and make an immediate attack. Forrest was reported crossing at Eastport to join the advance, with 15,000 men.

November 14th. Remained all day in camp. Details returned. All roads were effectually blockaded, in compliance with orders.

November 15th. The command moved out on the military road a few miles, toward Lawrenceburg, and camped at Wilcoxson's plantation.

November 16th, 17th and 18th. Still along the enemy's front, heavily picketing. The second brigade, Colonel Coon commanding, left the military road at eight o'clock, a.m., of the 16th, passed down the valley of Wolf Creek and crossed Shoal Creek at Wolf Ford, moved from the opposite side to Abberdeen, thence to Big Butler, and down to .Lit-tle Butler, from which place it moved directly south toward Wilson's Crossroads. After passing a mill the advance of the Second found the enemy's pickets and dashed at them furiously, running them into their reserve pell-mell, which created a stampede of the whole command, composed of General Rhoddy's brigade, which also ran back to their infantry camp in great confusion.

Through the gallant conduct of Lieutenant Tiffoth, company D, Second Iowa, the command captured several prisoners, who informed us of many important facts touching the movements of the enemy. After forcing Rhoddy within the infantry lines the brigade retraced their steps, re-crossing Shoal Creek at Savannah Ford, and went into camp at Harris's plantation, three miles from Cowpen's Mill. General Hatch became satisfied that the enemy were constantly receiving rein-

2ND BRIGADE 5TH CAVALRY DIVISION CHARGING REBEL WORKS AT NASHVILLE, DEC 13TH 1864

forcements, and that Forrest had recently joined Hood, (on the 14th,) and that the location about the two Butler creeks was not the most safe place for the camp of a cavalry command.

November 19th. While the first brigade was watching the different roads, the second brigade, Colonel Coon commanding, was ordered to move across Shoal Creek, at Cowpen's Ford, for the purpose of camping on Butler Creek. On reaching the creek, some three miles west, they drove in the enemy's pickets. Captain A. R. Mock, of the Ninth Illinois, commanding battalion, was sent to patrol the Waynesboro road—the main column to move north to Butler Creek, while Captain J. W. Harper, with the remainder of his regiment—the Ninth—stood picket on the road running south toward Florence. Colonel Coon and escort remained at the cross-roads to see the train safely closed up. He had not been superintending the direction of the train quite an hour when an orderly informed him that the Second had met the enemy in force, and that Buford's division (rebel) was in the front on Big Butler Creek.

At the same time Captain Harper reported the enemy pressing his pickets from the south, and had the appearance of being infantry. Leaving an orderly to close the column and sending another to inform Captain Harper that he must hold his position, at all hazards, until the pack-train and artillery had passed, as it was impossible, from the bad condition of the road, to halt or return by the same route, Colonel Coon rode rapidly to the Second Iowa, and found them engaged with a superior force. He at once sent an orderly with instructions for the train and artillery to turn up the valley of the Little Butler, accompanied by the Sixth Illinois as escort, Major Whitrish commanding, who was instructed to take all the spades and make a crossing on Shoal Creek, at all hazards, as this was the only place of escape from a well devised trap of the enemy.

Great anxiety was felt for the command, as Buford, on the north, was pressing the Second Iowa hard in front, and flanking on the right and left with vastly superior numbers, while the Ninth Illinois were heavily pressed in the rear by a force from the south. During this time a messenger was sent to Captain Mock, informing him that unless he returned soon the last place left for his escape would have to be abandoned.

As the Ninth Illinois came up they passed to the right and rear of the Second Iowa, down the Little Butler, and formed in line dismounted at the junction of the two rivers, where the high and abrupt bluffs on either side made the valley quite narrow. This made a good support for the Second when compelled to fall back. By this time the situation of the Second became critical, in consequence of the rapid movements of the rebel flanking column, which reached nearly to their rear on right and left.

Seeing that it was impossible to hold the gap until Captain Mock could be heard from, Major Horton was ordered to fall back and form again in rear of the Ninth Illinois; each regiment then fell back alternately and formed lines for two miles, when they reached Shoal Creek and found, to their great surprise, the Sixth Illinois pack-train, artillery and ambulances all safe on the other side, and the regiment dismounted to cover the crossing. A lively skirmish was kept up by the rear guard while the command passed down the steep, miry bank by file, obliquely, one hundred and fifty feet. The mortification and apparent chagrin of the rebels, when they found their prey had unexpectedly escaped their snare, was made known by their hideous yells, such as rebels only can make. Pickets were carefully placed on all practicable roads, and the command encamped at dark at the same place it left in the morning, with the firm belief that Butler Creek was by no means a desirable location to encamp. The day had been one of incessant rain.

November 20th. While the second brigade was engaged with the enemy, the first held a position a few miles below, and on the left of the Second, facing the enemy, while Croxton's brigade was posted yet further to the left of the first. The fighting devolved principally upon the second brigade. At three o'clock, a. m., the second moved out on the military road, thence to Bluewater Creek and camped, leaving pickets on the military road. Captain Mock, of the Ninth Illinois, reported on the military road, having travelled all night to reach the command. He succeeded in reaching the Waynesboro road, but in returning found himself and command completely surrounded by the enemy, and took to the hills by by-roads. By accident he came upon General Chalmers' division wagon-train, (rebel) made a charge on the guard, capturing several wagons and prisoners, and fifty mules, besides much plunder, which he could not bring away.

While in the act of destroying the train he was attacked by a superior force and compelled to leave all and take to the woods again. By the assistance of Union men and negroes he was guided by circuitous routes until he reached the column. His loss was thirty men, most of whom were taken prisoners. In capturing the train, papers conveying important information were found, which must have been of infinite importance to General Thomas, as they detailed the movements about to be made, giving timely notice to all of what was to take place. Captain Mock is entitled to much credit for the skill displayed in bringing out his command with so little loss. At sunset the pickets were driven in on the military road. Patrols who had been sent out returned, reporting the enemy advancing in force.

November 21st. The whole command moved at an early hour, on the Lexington road, the second brigade bringing up the rear. After resting a few hours at this place the whole force moved toward Lawrenceburg, the second brigade still guarding the rear. At five o'clock, p.m., the command reached the latter place and camped for the night. The day was cold, and much snow fell during the afternoon and night.

November 22nd. The morning was cold and the ground frozen hard. About twelve o'clock the enemy commenced skirmishing with our pickets, and Captain Bandy, Second Iowa, with one battalion, was sent to ascertain their force. After skirmishing with them an hour he returned and reported the enemy three miles from town in force, and strongly posted on bluffs and behind well arranged rail barricades. At two o'clock the enemy moved up in heavy force, infantry, cavalry and artillery, and encamped in line, in plain view of town and our bivouac. The general commanding the division ordered the second brigade into line of battle. A brisk artillery duel was kept up for an hour between the enemy and company K, First Illinois Artillery. In the meantime a large dismounted force was displayed, showing all the characteristics of infantry.

After holding the town until sundown the command was ordered to move out on the Pulaski road, Croxton's brigade in advance, while the second brought up the rear. The command withdrew in good order, though heavily pressed by superior numbers, and halted and camped seven miles east of Lawrenceburg.

November 23rd. Left camp at four o'clock in the morning, and halted at Richland Mills to feed and issue rations. General Croxton's command was in the rear, heavily skirmishing with the enemy. At three o'clock, p.m., the command moved three miles toward Pulaski, took up the valley of Dry Creek, and camped five miles south of Campbellville.

November 24th. Moved out at six o'clock, a.m., the second brigade bringing up the rear, and arrived at Campbellville at 9 o'clock. The patrols reported the enemy moving on our left, with videttes standing on every high bluff in sight. General Hatch ordered the patrols strengthened. Had proceeded but a short distance when an orderly arrived and reported that a heavy column (supposed to be Buford's division,) was in front of the first brigade. The second brigade was withdrawn and fell back to the east side of town, and held the Linnville roads until the first division, then in a critical situation, could be recalled. The second had no sooner taken position than the enemy's infantry made its appearance in heavy force on the south and west side of the town. The general ordered battery K, First Illinois, to commence firing, at a range of one and a half miles; the effect of the cannonading was excellent, causing the whole rebel column to halt for at least one hour.

During this time a flanking column of the enemy was discovered moving to our left, and threatening the Linnville road. The Second Iowa was immediately ordered to guard and check the movement, and they soon reported the force engaging them vastly superior to theirs. The Ninth Illinois was sent to their support. The position of these regiments soon became intolerable, as the enemy were undoubtedly moving their main column by the right flank, to get possession of the road in the rear. Upon learning this fact General Hatch ordered the second brigade to fall back and hold the road, regardless of the first. The enemy were strongly posted on the left of town, with a battery playing at one thousand yards. In the meantime the first brigade had succeeded, by flanking through the timber, passing over rugged and steep hills, and keeping up a bold front, in making a junction with the second. The Seventh Illinois, Major Graham commanding, made two gallant charges, driving the enemy before them in confusion. Two miles from Campbellville the flanking column and patrol of the second, from the left, were suddenly driven in.

As the road turned to the left, through a narrow gorge, and just at the time General Hatch was passing, Captain E. B. Phillips, company M, Sixth Illinois, commanding his escort, discovering the rebels, charged in an instant with his company and saved the gallant commander from being captured. This gallantry of Captain Phillips is worthy of special compliment here, as well for his daring as the good results. Unfortunately the captain received a wound in his left hand, which disabled him for the campaign.

The Ninth Illinois, Captain J. W. Harper commanding, followed immediately in rear of the escort, and were immediately ordered by him to dismount and hold the gap, at all hazards. Captain Harper had scarcely dismounted his men when they received a heavy fire from a brigade of the enemy; not a particle daunted the captain ordered his men forward until it became a hand-to-hand conflict. The captain received orders to fall back slowly, their ammunition—sixty rounds— being nearly exhausted. The Second Iowa was formed across the gorge to protect them while they withdrew. The loss of the Ninth in this fight was thirty killed and wounded, in as many minutes; among them were four orderly sergeants. Much credit is due Captain Harper for the skilful manner and good order in which he retreated, although the loss was heavy.

No sooner had the Ninth passed through the line of the Second Iowa than the rebel brigade came at a double-quick up the hollow, colours in front, and in another instant were in line of battle, when three hundred Spencer's in the hands of the Second Iowa drove them back in confusion; but a moment, however, intervened, when the rebels rallied. Major Horton, in the meantime, retired and mounted by battalions under fire, leaving one officer and five men on the field. The whole command then moved forward, Croxton in the advance, the second on the pike and the first to the left of the pike, while the rebels followed closely in the rear and on both flanks. At eleven o'clock, p.m., the command was in the rear of Columbia and inside the infantry pickets of the Fourth and Twenty-Third army corps, they being stationed there at that time.

November 25th. Crossed Duck River and camped three miles above the city. The advance of Hood's army was within a few miles of Columbia.

November 26th. At ten o'clock, a.m., moved out on the Murfreesboro road and camped eight miles east of Columbia. Hood's advance was engaged with our infantry. Rained constantly during the day and night.

November 27th. Remained in camp all day; raining very hard. The Seventh Illinois was assigned to the second brigade; Major John M. Graham, commanding the regiment, reported for duty. This transfer caused great rejoicing in the Seventh Illinois; they felt once more at home among their old comrades, with whom they had been previously brigaded. And now, kind reader, I will devote my pen almost

132

exclusively to the benefit of the second brigade, Col. Coon, commanding. I do not wish to slight other commands, who have acted nobly and bravely, but space will not permit me to dwell upon the good merits of all.

November 28th, Rained until noon. At 2 o'clock Colonel Coon received orders to move immediately. While boots and saddles were being sounded the enemy opened with a volley upon the pickets on the Shelbyville road. By the aid of a glass the enemy could be seen in heavy force through the thin fog, about two miles distant. Captain Foster, commanding battalion of Second Iowa, was ordered to support the pickets while the command made preparations to move. By direction of the general commanding the artillery was sent to Hunt's Cross-Roads, on the Lewisburg pike, where the brigade erected a slight barricade of rails, and slept on their arms during the night.

November 29th. The brigade took up its line of march at four o'clock, a.m., passing Croxton's and Harrison's commands, and moving toward Franklin. The second brigade marched in the rear of the division to Mount Carmel, when it halted and fell in line of battle to the left of the pike. At 9 o'clock, a.m., General Croxton's command passed, heavily pressed by the enemy. The light rail barricade, previously constructed, served as a temporary breastwork, and enabled the second, then dismounted, to check the enemy's movements. But a few moments passed until the whole line was engaged in a heavy skirmish, which continued for an hour, when they were ordered to withdraw slowly, which was done by alternate numbers in line for two miles; the brigade was then ordered to mount and withdraw by brigade in line of regiments, each regiment in line of squadrons, in columns of fours.

The enemy discovering this formation charged down the pike, in column of fours, on a small company of the Ninth Illinois, who were acting as rear-guard. The company did not halt, but continued to fall back, leading the enemy between the flanking column right and left, who opened upon them a raking fire, throwing them into confusion, and ending the pursuit for the day. The command arrived at Knowland's plantation, at twelve o'clock, and halted in line of battle until four o'clock, p.m., when it moved toward Franklin two miles, and turning to the right crossed Little Harworth River and moved north to the Knowlandsville and Franklin road, where the brigade camped for the night.

November 30th. The Twelfth Tennessee Cavalry, Colonel R. R.

Spaulding, commanding, was this day assigned to the second brigade, and reported for duty. The day was a beautiful one. The positions on the roads were held in quiet until about three o'clock, p.m. The enemy had previously skirmished General Croxton's command heavily, which was picketing the river, and at this hour compelled him to give back. The Confederate cavalry on their right made a general attack on the Federal cavalry on Schofield's left, and simultaneously with their main assault on the Federal works at Franklin, with the evident design of forcing back and flanking General Schofield's position. General Hatch formed a portion of the Twelfth Tennessee, a detachment of the Tenth Tennessee, the Third, Sixth, Ninth and Seventh in order from right to left, and facing a high ridge to the south, with the Second Iowa thrown across the Knowlandsville road half a mile east of and at right-angles with the main line, all dismounted. The fight was a very simple and brief one; heavy skirmishing well up with his right, and exchanged some pretty heavy firing.

The general ordered his line to charge; he was then on the left with the Seventh Illinois, which wound up a long hill, in a direction to detach it by opening both flanks from its support, and upon gaining the brow of the hill unmasking a heavy line of dismounted men, carrying their stands of colors. With a volley and a cheer it charged them, driving them through their bivouac and across the river, and they were still retreating when this regiment was recalled. The regiments to the right joined in the advance, and carried the hill in their front, driving the enemy in most gallant style until they had recrossed the Little Harworth.

Our cavalry on the Knowlandsville road was not attacked. The enemy's forces were estimated at from five to six thousand strong, and were said to be Buford's division of cavalry and mounted infantry. The entire brigade acquitted itself in a most creditable manner, and camped for the night on the ground occupied the night previous. From this date no operation of importance transpired, save the march to Nashville, occupying the 1st, when the command skirmished a little at Brentwood's, and the 2nd, when it marched at five o'clock, and arrived in the vicinity of Fort Negley about eight o'clock the same morning. Until the 12th the time was diligently employed in re-furnishing the command. On the 13th it crossed the river and camped near the defence.

December 15th. By order of Gen. Hatch, pursuant to orders from

Brevet Maj.-Gen. Wilson, commanding cavalry corps M. D. M., the division and brigade was marched at an early hour from camp, crossing the field on the right of the Harding pike, in the following order: The second brigade on the right of the infantry, commanded by Maj.-Gen. A. J. Smith, Sixteenth army corps, and on the left of the first brigade, with its regiments from right to left, the Twelfth Tennessee, mounted, Seventh Illinois, Second Iowa, Sixth and Seventh Illinois, dismounted, with horses led in the rear, and men carrying one day's rations and one hundred rounds of ammunition per man. The other cavalry extended the line to the Cumberland River on the right, and its movement was by a grand left-wheel against the enemy to double up his left, and by driving his centre in to concentrate the Federal attack, besides opening a way to his rear, if it should be advantageous to use it.

The rapidity of the movements of the infantry upon the left, and which constituted the movable pivot of the grand left-wheel of the cavalry, was so rapid that it was found impossible to accelerate the movements on the right. To keep up the entire line the various divisions and even brigades became separated, and even detached, and when the second brigade finally went into close action the first brigade on its right was detached some miles. It was down this opening that the Twelfth Tennessee, Colonel R. R. Spaulding, commanding, charged and captured some twenty wagons and teams, about forty-five prisoners, and a large amount of plunder, belonging to the rebel General Chalmers' headquarters.

By one o'clock we had rolled back the enemy successively from the Charlotte, Hardin and Broad Street pikes, and approached some of the rebel redoubts, with the brigade line facing nearly due east, and much in advance of the infantry, which was moving down from the north. The brigade being formed on the extreme right of the infantry caused lively marching for the men, as the distance travelled by them was much further than that of the infantry; for three miles the marching was done on a double-quick. After a sharp artillery duel for an hour between the first redoubt and battery I, First Illinois Light Artillery, attached to the division, the brigade was ordered to charge the redoubts containing the guns.

The regiments engaged in this charge were the Seventh Illinois, Major John M. Graham commanding, on the right, with the Second Iowa, Major C. C. Horton, and Ninth Illinois, Captain J. W. Harper commanding, in order on its left, and the Sixth Illinois, Lieut.-Col. John Lynch commanding, on the left of the brigade. In making this charge the right wing of the brigade—Seventh Illinois and Second Iowa—had an open field, with nothing to impede their progress save two stone fences, while the left wing—Ninth and Sixth Illinois—had a heavy thicket to pass through. At the word "forward," stone fences and thickets were very slight impediments in the way of this veteran brigade. At the distance of about eight hundred yards southwest of the work assaulted was another redoubt, mounting two guns, and filled with several hundred infantry; from this latter work, while moving eastward on the first, the Second Iowa and Seventh Illinois were exposed to a continuous shower of shells and musketry.

The right of the Seventh Illinois, who were not more than four hundred yards from it, giving first their front, then their right flank, then their rear to this fire, without shrinking for a moment or firing a shot, was as proud evidence of good soldiership as ever displayed. The enemy in the first redoubt, discovering the movements, changed their little messengers (shells) to grape and canister, accompanied by heavy musketry from the infantry support behind their works. The men never halted from the time the charge was sounded until they had possession of the works, containing four Napoleon guns and seventy-five prisoners, besides a large number of small arms, thrown away by the enemy in their rapid flight. So eager were the men of each regiment to reach the redoubt first, that they became mixed up in such a manner that it is a difficult question to settle, or say who was first to reach the prize.

All acted nobly, and all are entitled to the highest praise, under the circumstances, for their efforts to be first. The Second Iowa planted the first colours on the works; the others had none with them. General Hatch was among the first to reach the redoubt, and he is under the impression that Lieutenant Budd was the first officer inside the works, and consequently ordered him to take command of the guns and use them immediately upon the retreating enemy, which order was carried out with good effect. In the capture of this redoubt the infantry were behind time, though they afforded good support, and were fully as anxious to gain the prize as were the cavalry. After its surrender a major of an Ohio infantry regiment mounted the works, drew his sword and claimed the honour of capturing the fort for his regiment, but the cavalrymen standing around cooled his ardour.

The rebel colours, which lay on the ground folded up, had been overlooked by our cavalry, and were afterward found by some infantry belonging to General McArthur's division. But few of the men lingered to view what they had captured—each and all were eager in the pursuit of the retreating foe, and were continually bringing them in by squads, numbering from two to forty. Major Forbes, Seventh Illinois, states that he met one sergeant and two privates in charge of thirty prisoners. The rally being sounded General Hatch ordered a charge to be made on redoubt number two, which had not ceased to fire its deadly missies. With General Hatch and Colonel Coon at their head the men charged, and in less than thirty minutes after the order was given the works were in the possession of our brave cavalrymen.

This redoubt was situated upon the top of a bluff, some two hundred feet high, and protected by strong earthworks. The colours of the Second Iowa were planted on the works by Sergeant John Hartman, of company F, colour-bearer, who fell mortally wounded, and a braver man never faced the enemy. His last words were spoken to Major Horton, requesting him to tell his friends at home that he fell while performing his duty. During the charge the enemy kept up a brisk cannonading, accompanied by heavy musketry firing from the infantry within the redoubt. The long march previous, the charge on the first redoubt, and the short time given until the second charge, rendered it almost impossible for a cavalryman to move faster than a walk. So eager were the officers and men to reach the second redoubt that many fell to the ground exhausted. Lieut.-Col. John Lynch, commanding the Sixth Illinois, fell exhausted and was carried from the field. Many soldiers, when too tired to walk, crawled upon their hands and knees up the steep bluff to the foot of the redoubt.

While the cavalry were rallying for the second charge General Hatch was apprised by Major Forbes, Seventh Illinois, of a very threatening movement of the enemy, who were concentrating a considerable force in a ravine in the edge of the wood, to the east of and at right-angles with the main pike, with the evident design of attacking the left of our main line, then moving westward against the second redoubt. The general at once comprehended the design of the enemy, and turning to the major said, "Go into them, sir, with what you've got." The major started for them at the head of about twenty-five men of his own regiment, and a few members of the Second Iowa cavalry and Fifth Minnesota infantry, not more than forty men in all; they charged and drove fully three hundred rebels from a greatly superior position, pursuing them three-quarters of a mile, and returned with ninety prisoners; meanwhile from the captured redoubt went up three hearty cheers for Uncle Sam.

A rather amusing incident occurred while charging this redoubt, which was told me by an officer of high standing in this brigade. As the gallant General Hatch was charging up the hill, leading his command, his attention was attracted toward a cavalryman, a member of the Ninth Illinois, who was lying on the ground trying to crawl up the hill; but so exhausted was the poor fellow that it was impossible for him to go any further without some assistance. The general asked him what ailed him; he stated the fact, when the general told him to get hold of his horse's tail, and hold on, and he would help him up the hill, which was done. Another dispute arose as to who was the first to enter the fort, every regiment claiming the honour. The fort surrendered to Captain McCausland, and it was difficult, to restrain the men from firing upon the rebels after they surrendered.

Among some of the first to enter this fort was an infantryman, who had pushed ahead of his command and joined the cavalry, eager for the fun. He was a fine looking fellow, and with his bayonet fixed he kept close behind the captain, and as the latter demanded the surrender of the fort exclaimed, "Go it captain; I will follow you to h—l on a charge!" In this redoubt when captured were two twelve-pound guns, a large quantity of ammunition, over one hundred prisoners, including one surgeon, one major, and one captain. The infantry were behind time, unable to keep up with the cavalry, who did not keep very good order, while the former moved in solid column. It was very mortifying to them, and you could hear their officers calling upon the men to hurry up, and not let the cavalrymen take all the forts, which feat not only surprised them, but when it was reported to Maj.-Gen. Thomas that the cavalry had carried the first works, he replied, "Tut, tut, impossible, impossible, sir; such a thing as cavalrymen carrying forts by assault has never been heard of."

However the general was convinced of the fact, by witnessing the brigade enter the second redoubt. The cavalry were soon in hot pursuit of the retreating rebels, leaving the fort and prisoners in charge of the infantry. It was now getting dark. Colonel Coon, mistaking two regiments of the first brigade for his own, had the honour of leading them to the summit of a third hill, under a most galling fire from the enemy in front and on both flanks, and holding the position until the infantry support came up, when they charged, driving the enemy before them and capturing three pieces of artillery.

The colonel says he will ever remember with pleasure the gallant conduct of the officers and men of the two regiments, which he had been told were the Twelfth Missouri and Eleventh Indiana cavalry regiments. At dark the brigade went into camp near the redoubts, on the Lewisburg pike.

December 16th. At ten o'clock, a.m., the brigade was ordered out to support General Nipe, commanding division of cavalry. After advancing one mile the brigade moved to the east of the pike, and formed a line dismounted, then moved forward in conformity to the infantry toward the Granny White pike. The steep hills, rising abruptly from one to two hundred feet high, and covered with a thick undergrowth, made it almost impossible to manoeuvre troops, even when dismounted. The regiments were in line of order as on the preceding day, each upon a hill. After moving forward nearly one mile the whole line became engaged.

During the first hour the Seventh Illinois came upon a brigade of rebel infantry, strongly posted. A charge was at once ordered by Major Graham, commanding, who immediately after fell, wounded in the arm, and was carried from the field. The command now devolved upon Major Henry C. Forbes, who led the charge then in progress, and was ably sustained by the third battalion, under Captain McCausland, who, a few moments after, fell wounded—a young, brave and efficient officer, loved and admired by the regiment for his many noble qualities. The command moved up the hill in a direction perpendicular to the movements on the right, when the enemy gave way, throwing their guns in every direction and surrendering seventy-two prisoners, including a captain and four lieutenants.

The position thus gallantly taken was untenable for a single regiment. The enemy rallied upon discovering the small force that attacked them, and this regiment was obliged to withdraw, which it did in good order, bringing away the prisoners, and destroying the arms captured, by breaking and bending the barrels. Had the regiment been supported by any portion of the brigade they would have succeeded in making a large capture. The regiment lost fifteen men, killed and wounded, during the fight, including four officers. The same ground was passed over a few hours afterward by the remainder of the brigade, the enemy having evacuated the position.

During the afternoon the Sixth and Ninth Illinois, with the Second Iowa, were engaged firing at will on a fort some five hundred yards distant, while Battery I, First Illinois Light Artillery, played upon it from the valley below, which soon caused the enemy to evacuate. The line moved forward and the Twelfth Tennessee Cavalry charged and captured one hundred and fifty prisoners, eight stand of colours which were left in the hands of the infantry.

The enemy were retreating in great haste on the Granny White pike. The brigade was ordered to charge them, if possible, before dark. Col. Spaulding, of the Twelfth Tennessee, took the advance, and had not proceeded more than a mile when he made a charge which threw them into confusion, and by the assistance of the Ninth Illinois, who were brought up dismounted, drove them from a strong position protected by a barricade of rails; the Twelfth Tennessee, Sixth and Ninth Illinois followed them to another strong position, a half mile distant, when a hand to hand fight took place and lasted an hour after dark.

At this place Brig.-Gen. Bucker was captured by Captain Joseph Boyer, Twelfth Tennessee Cavalry, who received a severe blow on the forehead at the hand of the rebel general. In that personal contest Captain Boyer wrenched the rebel General's sabre from his hand, who in turn seized and took his; several cuts and points were executed by both parties, each one exhibiting skill in the use of their weapons; by a powerful and dexterous blow Captain Boyer succeeded in knocking from the general's hand his sword; the general then put spurs to his horse and tried to escape, upon which the captain drew his revolver and shot him through the arm, which resulted in his capture.

It was in this *mêlée*, amidst intense darkness, that the two regiments of Twelfth Tennessee Cavalry (Federal and Confederate) met and mixed in mad confusion, neither knowing the other save by the usual challenge, "halt! who comes there?" Colonel Spaulding who was foremost in the charge was halted by two Confederate soldiers, who, on hearing his answer to the challenge grasped his horse by the reins on either side and demanded his surrender; the colonel put spurs to his horse and with one bound the noble animal took himself and rider beyond danger. Private Barny Watson, Company G, Twelfth Tennessee, captured and brought away General Bucker's division flag, and was promoted to sergeant the same night for his gallant conduct. Majors Corwin and Bradshaw of the Twelfth Tennessee charged entirely through the rebel lines with their battalions and afterward returned by passing themselves off as belonging to the Twelfth Tennessee, (Confederate Cavalry,) and in great anxiety to meet the Yankees. The brigade encamped for the night on Granny White's pike, eight miles south of Nashville.

December 17th. Moved at daylight and continued the pursuit, following in the rear of the enemy's cavalry to Franklin, and thence to the Louisburgh pike, and crossed over to the Columbia pike. When three miles south of Franklin the enemy were met in force. The whole brigade was formed and charged, mounted, driving in the rebel left. The Second Iowa pressed their way round to the rebel left and rear, where they became engaged in a hand to hand fight, resulting in the capture of one stand of colours and several prisoners. In this engagement Sergeant John Coulter, Corporal A. R. Heck and private Black, of company K, Second Iowa, captured a stand of Division colours. The two latter were killed and the former severely wounded—but he succeeded in bringing away the colours. So desperate had been the conflict for these colours that two Federals and three Confederates lay dead within three paces of each other.

The firing in the rear, in conjunction with the brisk engagement in front, caused the enemy to fall back. General Hatch, with small detachments from the Sixth, Seventh and Ninth Illinois and Second Iowa, made a most gallant charge, which resulted in the capture of three more pieces of artillery, (formerly the famous Waterhouse Battery, of Chicago, captured from General Sturgis, by Forrest, near Gumtown, Mississippi, June, 1864.) The darkness of the night prevented further movements and the brigade went into camp, seven miles below Franklin.

December 18th. Continued the pursuit to Spring Hill, where a considerable force of the enemy were found. After firing a few shots, they fell back in confusion. The brigade camped three miles south of Spring Hill.

December 19th. Resumed the march to Rutherford's Creek, where the command dismounted and marched by the right flank. The Sixth Illinois succeeded in crossing the wreck of the burned railroad bridge, when the fragments floated away and the balance of the command were compelled to ford the stream some distance above. Moved two miles below the enemy's flank, the Sixth skirmishing until dark, when the command encamped for the night.

December 20th. At daylight were again in motion. Moved down Rutherford's Creek, about two miles, and constructed a crossing from the fragments of a railroad bridge, which the enemy had destroyed the day previous. This work was soon completed, and by twelve o'clock the whole command was across. The Seventh and Ninth were dismounted and deployed on foot, while the remainder of the brigade followed mounted to Duck River, opposite Columbia.

On arriving at Columbia they found that the enemy had crossed his rear guard in safety that morning, leaving a small party, with a piece of artillery, to guard the town, upon the opposite side. A brisk skirmish was kept up for some time, between the enemy's sharpshooters, who were lodged in the buildings. At the same time a light artillery duel was going on. General Hatch at once turned his attention toward the sharpshooters and ordered the buildings shelled, which soon caused an evacuation of them, and, also, an interview with General Forrest, who appeared with a flag of truce and approached the water's edge, requesting General Hatch not to shell the town, as he was doing more injury to his own men (many of whom lay in the buildings wounded) than theirs.

General Hatch replied that he would stop the shelling if he—General Forrest—would withdraw the sharpshooters—which was done. At the conclusion General Forrest remarked to General Hatch that he hoped he would see him again. The general replied, that he hoped he would have that pleasure. During the skirmish the Seventh discovered where the enemy had abandoned four pieces of artillery, by tumbling them into Duck River. They were afterward taken out by the infantry.

December 21st, 22nd and 23rd were occupied pursuing the retreating enemy, continually bringing in prisoners, wagons, ambulances, caissons, small arms, &c. The road was literally strewn with arms, blankets, knapsacks, cartridge-boxes, &c. One battalion of the Second Iowa, under Captain G.W. Foster, company M, was sent on the Shelbyville pike, in pursuit of a party of rebels who were reported escaping, with two pieces of artillery. The captain succeeded in capturing them, after a day's march, and also found six ambulances and three wagons. The enemy, on the 23rd, camped five miles south of Columbia, on the Pulaski pike. Prisoners reported that they had orders when they discovered Hatch's division pressing their rear not to fire but one shot before limbering up.

It was a stated fact that if the enemy attempted to fire more than one round our men would charge and capture the guns. They asserted that they never saw such men; they did not seem to care anything about their artillery fire, but seemed to take delight in charging their guns, and would only stop to take aim and fire, not stopping to load nary a time—showing the superiority of the Spencer carbine.

December 24th. Brigade had some sharp skirmishing with Buford's

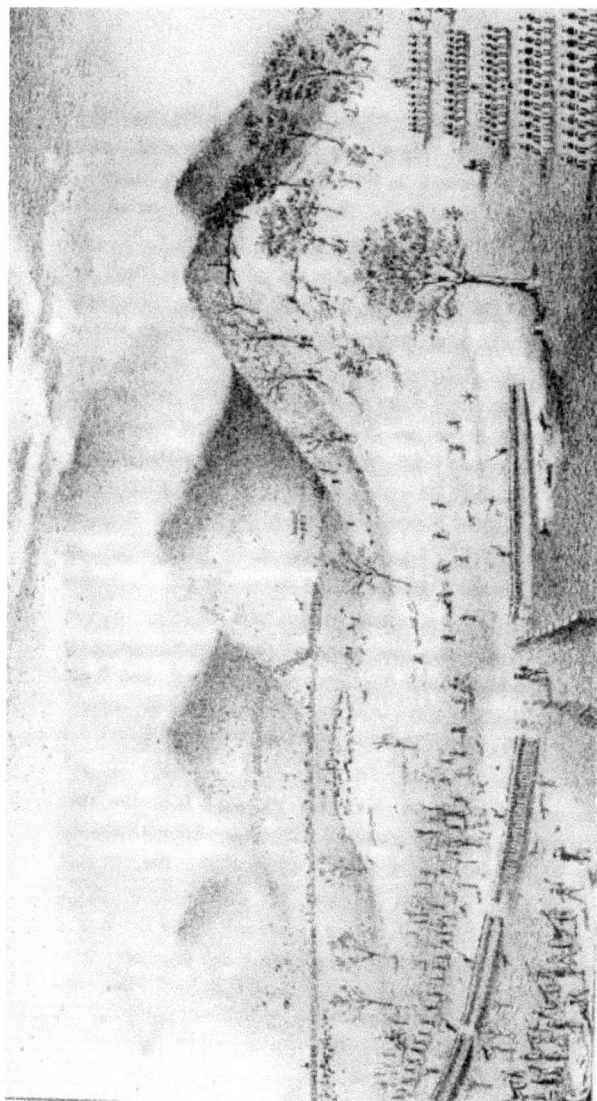

Charge of 2nd Brigade 3rd Cavalry Division on rebel forts at Nashville, 1864

division, and the rebel General Buford was wounded by the Seventh Illinois sharpshooters.

December 25th. Brigade marched in rear of General Hammond and Colonel Harrison's commands, passing beyond Pulaski, some six miles, where the enemy were found in force. Harrison's command being badly repulsed the Second brigade was ordered forward, dismounted. After a skirmish of an hour they drove the enemy from a strong position and camped for the night.

December 26th. From this date little fighting was done. The enemy had crossed the Tennessee at Bainbridge, badly defeated and terribly demoralized.

After a period of hard marching to Gravelly Springs, Alabama, the command went into camp, and remained three weeks, subsisting about two-thirds of the time on parched corn—owing to the scarcity of rations at the time. At the same time boats were constantly arriving loaded with forage, necessitating a great amount of fatigue duty. This, together with the inferior diet, caused much sickness among the men. However, General Hatch was not to blame for this gross neglect of the men, as he was subject to orders from superior officers.

During the stay of the command at Gravelly Springs, scouting parties were frequently sent out. On one occasion company A, Seventh Illinois Cavalry, Lieut. J. I. LaGrange commanding, (to whom I am indebted for the following items,) states that, returning from Waterloo to Athens, a rebel deserter, John Mitchel, belonging to the First Missouri battery, came to us on the road, gave himself up, stating that he was tired of the war, and wished to get to his home in Missouri. He said that he had been in the rebel service nearly four years, and participated in every battle of any consequence in the west, commencing with the battle of Frederickstown, Missouri, and ending with Hood's defeat at Nashville, and that during all the engagements between the two mentioned, Chickamaugua included, he never saw men fight with the cool, calm, determined bravery of Hatch's cavalry. "Why, d—n it," says he, "you all must have been drunk or mad, for you paid no more attention to our batteries throwing solid shot, shell, grape, and canister at you than you would at a four year old boy throwing stones, and every stand our battery made—and it was kept continually in the rear—we would never have an opportunity to fire over four rounds before you all would be upon us, and we would be compelled to limber up and get out at a gallop, to save our pieces.

It is the first time during my four years of almost continual fighting that my old battery ever failed to repulse a charge, and she has been 'went for' frequently. And you can judge whether or not I have seen any service when I tell you upon the honour of a soldier, that I am the only man left out of a regiment of seven hundred that was organized in April, 1861. There was seven of us at the Battle of Franklin, but upon going over the ground at daylight the next morning after the fearful and deadly charge of the day before, I saw (and the tears rolled down the cheeks of the noble fellow as he said it) my six companions lying stark and cold, and you now see before you, to the best of my knowledge, the only living representative of that seven hundred men. And now I am going home, satisfied that the South can never gain her independence, and to try and find the friends at I have not seen, or even heard from, for over three years."

The following order was issued, and read on dress parade, at the head of each regiment.

Headquarters Second Brigade, Fifth Division, C. C.,
Gravelly Springs, Ala., M. D. M.,
January 31st, 1865.

General Field Orders No. 2:

The colonel commanding takes this, the first opportunity, to express to the officers and men of this brigade his heartfelt thanks for their untiring energy and loyal, devoted patriotism to their country's cause, during the recent arduous campaign. He feels confident that the labours performed, and suffering endured, through rain, sleet and snow overhead, and mud underfoot, while at Shoal Creek, the retreat to Nashville; the cold, bleak weather at Edgefield, followed by the two days' battle at Nashville and near Franklin; the cold storm at Rutherford's Creek, and in the pursuit to the Tennessee River, are without parallel in the history of this war, while your record of gallantry and bravery has been more brilliant than that of any other cavalry brigade in the United States' service.

You have done what your noble department commander said could not be done with cavalry. When a staff officer reported that General Hatch's cavalry had charged and taken a fort, he replied, "Impossible, impossible, sir! such a thing was never heard of." When he and his staff rode forward rapidly to ascertain the truth of this report, arriving at the first redoubt in time to witness your taking the second, with no little astonishment. You have won for yourselves and your respective States immortal fame; you have taught the army and the world the important lesson that cavalry can fight and charge breastworks, on foot, a fact heretofore almost unknown.

The acts of personal bravery during the campaign have been numerous, too many to mention here, but all present know who those men are, and you will do important service by relating, in the presence of "skulkers," the incidents of gallant conduct in the recent engagements.

The brigade now has a name truly enviable, and it is hoped that no officer or soldier will fail to lend his entire energy to render the record still more brilliant. Let our motto be: *First in drill; first in discipline; unsurpassed in soldierly conduct, and, as of late, foremost in every battle.*

By command of

Datus E. Coon,

Colonel Second Iowa Cavalry, Commanding Brigade.

John H. Avery,

Lieut. Ninth Ill. Cav., and A. A. A. G.

From Gravelly Springs the command moved to Eastport, Mississippi, and engaged in recruiting up, preparatory to another grand move.

In conclusion, I must say the campaign and labours of the brigade have been endured by the officers and men with unparalleled fortitude. They have been subject to all the privations that soldiers are heir to, and without eliciting the least complaint. An army made of such materials, veterans of nearly four years' standing, can accomplish what the world never before witnessed.

I would do an injustice were I to omit mentioning the important service rendered this brigade by company I, First Illinois Light Artillery, Lieutenant Joseph McCarteny, commanding, from the time it reported at Nashville up to the present, and especially in the battle of Nashville, on the 15th and 16th of December, and in every action and engagement the men and officers conducted themselves in a cool, brave and gallant style, always delivering their messengers to the enemy with astonishing accuracy.

The Regimental Surgeons, (of whom Dr. Riggs, Seventh Illinois; Dr. Burgess, Assistant Surgeon, Second Iowa; Dr. Agnew, Assistant Surgeon, Sixth Illinois; Dr. Jones, Assistant Surgeon Twelfth Tennessee; Dr. Price, Assistant Surgeon, Ninth Illinois; Dr. Corbusin, Acting Assistant Surgeon Ninth Illinois,) whose labours were unremitting during the tedious marches and on every battlefield, to the sick and wounded, and to their care many are indebted for life and limb.

During the charges on the first and second redoubts the Brigade Band, consisting of sixteen pieces, belonging to the Second Iowa and Sixth Illinois, played patriotic airs, which enlivened the men. They then did duty in carrying and caring for the wounded.

The following names comprise the field and staff of Brevet Maj.-Gen. Edward Hatch, commanding the Fifth Division Cavalry Corps, Military Department of the Mississippi.

Captain Hervy A. Calvin, Twelfth Tennessee Cavalry and A. A. G.

Major E. T. Phillips, Sixth Illinois Cavalry and P. M.

Surgeon J. S. Hunt, Third Illinois Cavalry and Surgeon in Chief of Division.

Captain J. P. Metcalf, Second Iowa Cavalry and A. A. I. G.

Captain Wm. B. Brunton, Second Iowa Cavalry and A. O. O.

Captain R. Ken. Martin, Eleventh Indiana Cavalry and A. A. Chief of Musters.

Captain F. W. Babooqe:, Sixth Illinois Cavalry and commanding escort.

First Lieutenant Paul R. Kendall, Twelfth Missouri Cavalry and A. A. Q. M.

First Lieutenant E. A. Devenport, Ninth Illinois Cavalry and A.C.S.

The following names comprise the field and staff of Brevet Brig.-Gen. Datus E. Coon, commanding Second Brigade of the Fifth Division Cavalry Corps, Military Department of the Mississippi.

Major Geo. B. Christy, Ninth Illinois Cavalry and Senior Surgeon of the Brigade.

Captain John H. Avery, Ninth Illinois Cavalry and A. A. A. G.

Captain Geo. W. Budd, Second Iowa Cavalry and A. A. I. G.

First Lieutenant H. B. Sudlow, Second Iowa Cavalry and A.A.Q.M.

First Lieutenant Jas. Price, Seventh Illinois Cavalry and A. O. commanding escort.

Farewell Orders

FAREWELL ORDER OF MAJ.-GEN, EDWARD HATCH

Headquarters District of Talladega,
Talladega, Ala., Aug. 23, 1865.

General Orders, No. 4

Orders have this day been received directing me to report to another department for duty, which compel me to part with the officers and men of the Second Regiment Cavalry, Iowa Veteran Volunteers, and the Sixth, Seventh and Ninth Regiments Cavalry, Illinois Veteran Volunteers, with whom I have been so long and so pleasantly associated.

There are times in the course of events when the best of friends must part, and now that the hour of our separation draws nigh, I desire to express my sincere and heartfelt thanks for the cheerful co-operation with me in the performance of kindred duties, for your gallantry, self-denial, and untiring energy you have displayed on every occasion while under my command.

Participation in common dangers, privations and hardships, for nearly four years—a period too full of events and heroic deeds that you have accomplished to be mentioned in an order like this—has united us in the bond of an indissoluble friendship.

Often during your military career have you nobly obeyed the command: "Charge the enemy's works!" even amid volleys of iron hail and leaden rain, delivered by a brave and confident enemy. No greater praise can be offered than the fact that you have never charged a work you have not carried—a line you have not broken—or a battery you have not taken.

I will ever cherish, among the brightest passages of my life, the memory of our association while engaged in a cause in behalf of right against wrong and oppression. And now that the war is over, and we are spared to enjoy the fruits of our labours, let us not forget our comrades in arms, whose remains were left on the field of battle, or those who have been stricken down by the slow hand of disease; but let their sacred memory renew our devotion to the cause for which they gave their last offering.

You have done your duty as good soldiers, and each one of you have my best wishes for your future welfare and happiness, throughout the remainder of your lives.

Hoping the future may be as bright and prosperous as your military life has been glorious, I bid you an affectionate goodbye.

Edward Hatch,

Brevet Major-General Commanding.

FAREWELL ORDER OF BREVET BRIG,-GEN, COON,

Headquarters 2nd Brigade, 5th Div. C. C. M. D. M.,

Decatur, Ala., July 9th, 1865.

General Orders, No. 11.

Veteran companions! This day the identity of the old Second Brigade is lost, and its unflinching battle line, that covered our retreating forces at West Point and Prairie Station that saved a disorganized command at Okolona—that raised the well earned battle-cry of "victory!" at Hurricane Creek and Tupelo that presented its unbroken front to Hood's advancing hosts at Shoal Creek, Mt. Carmel, Campbelville, Linnville, Louisburg Pike and Franklin—and that taught the world a new lesson in cavalry warfare when it waved its victorious battle-flags over the captured redoubts at Nashville—that unwavering, battle-scarred line has at last, by order of your department commander, been broken. And in parting I feel proud in giving expression to the heart-felt "Godspeeds," and sincere "well-wishes," mutually exchanged by the officers and men of the brigade.

You have endured storm, hunger, fatigue, and disaster; and enjoyed sunshine, plenty, and many a victorious march together. Under each other's faithful watch you have slept without fear in many a dangerous bivouac. Shoulder to shoulder you have stemmed the battle tide on many a sanguinary field, and the greatest good I could wish for you is that your future happiness and prosperity may be as great and unremitting as your past patriotism, fidelity and courage while better cause for honest pride I shall never possess than this: I once commanded the Second Brigade. Officers, soldiers, comrades, farewell!

By order of

Datus E. Coon,

Brevet Brigadier-General.
John H. Avery,
Capt. and A. A. A. G.
To commanding officer Seventh Illinois Cavalry.

www.ingramcontent.com/pod-product-compliance
Lightning Source LLC
Chambersburg PA
CBHW021005090426
42738CB00007B/660